ENGAGING RESEARCH

HOLLY HANSEN-THOMAS
SERIES EDITOR

TRANSFORMING PRACTICES
for the
HIGH SCHOOL CLASSROOM

Mandy Stewart and
Holly Hansen-Thomas, Editors

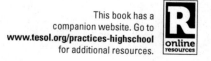

This book has a
companion website. Go to
www.tesol.org/practices-highschool
for additional resources.

www.tesol.org/bookstore

TESOL International Association
1925 Ballenger Avenue
Alexandria, Virginia, 22314 USA
www.tesol.org

Director of Publishing and Product Development: Myrna Jacobs
Copy Editor: Tomiko Breland
Cover: Citrine Sky Design
Interior Design and Layout: Capitol Communications, LLC
Printing: Gasch Printing, LLC

ISBN 978-1-942799-50-4

Library of Congress Control Number 2017953914

TABLE OF CONTENTS

Section 3: Science

Section 4: Mathematics

Series Editor's Preface

As English language educators, we value research for its benefit in providing evidence-based knowledge in our understanding of how English as a second or foreign language is learned (or acquired) by our students. Research also provides insight on best practices for teaching. But such research is only useful insofar as it is practical for teachers in classroom settings. It is necessary to translate, and indeed, *transform* conceptual and empirical research into practical and applicable information so that it can be used to evoke positive change for teachers and learners. That is, engaging with research is critical for practicing teachers.

TESOL International Association's research agenda (2014) promotes one issue very relevant to engaging research. One of its six bullet points maintains that the agenda intends to "promote dialog between doers and users of research" (p. 1). Furthermore, the agenda maintains that "because research is sometimes viewed as activity that generates knowledge but which has little relevance to everyday practice, (it) calls for more attention on how practitioners can use research" (p. 2). It is this grounding on which the current series is rooted.

The main goal of this series is to create new spaces for practitioner knowledge and engagement with English language teaching (ELT) research. As a professional community, we are interested in highlighting how ELT practitioners direct their own learning through reading, questioning, interpreting, and adapting research findings to and in their own contexts. Understanding and accessing original research in the field is critically important for teachers of all levels, and busy ELT professionals may not always have the opportunity or inclination to spend time reading and digesting academic journals or theory-based texts. As such, this series serves ELT practitioners by providing nuggets of original research from TESOL publications in the form of rich and detailed synopses. Further, each chapter puts the original highlighted research into practice by providing a replicable lesson plan and a reflection on its implementation, so teachers will have an idea of how such a lesson plays out in certain contexts. The result is a very accessible and rich collection that adds to the profession's overall knowledge base, while also validating the critical role teachers play in TESOL's overall mission to improve learning and teaching. The series recasts a great amount of ELT material from *TESOL Journal*, TESOL Quarterly, *Essential Teacher*, and other TESOL Press publications, such as the English Language Teaching in Context series.

There are four books in the series, with each book following a similar format. Three of the books cover the elementary, middle school, and high school levels and have chapters dedicated to the content areas of mathematics, science, social studies, and English language arts. There is also a volume devoted to English as a foreign language, and it is divided into three parts: primary, secondary, and higher education. The series is published in print, but resources, interactive links, and supplementary materials are available for download on a website dedicated to the series. In this way, teachers have ready access to multiple resources for their classrooms.

A benefit of the series stems from the diversity of classrooms and teachers represented in each volume. The individual chapters speak to the various educational profiles of students in diverse regions. As a result, the chapters highlight English learners (ELs) hailing from various linguistic and cultural backgrounds throughout the United States and beyond, as well as teachers with varying content and training backgrounds. Accordingly, academic and language standards for lesson plans correspond to the location and context in which each chapter is set. Among others, readers see Common Core State Standards for content, standards specific to particular states, and language standards, such as WIDA. This makes for a comprehensive and wide-ranging collection of classroom lessons.

The chapters follow a similar format for ease of use. To begin, each chapter provides a brief introduction that highlights the focal topic of the original research and the lesson plan, and background on the context, such as the school, student demographics, content area, and language and grade levels of students. Next follows a synopsis of the original research article or chapter, including the original citation. Then, authors include their rationale for choosing the research and creating a lesson based on it. Each chapter next highlights a clearly written lesson plan that allows readers to experience the context and follow the development of the lesson as it unfolds. To maintain continuity, ease of use, and readability, each lesson includes similar components to include the grade and subject area, content and language objectives, connections to appropriate standards, desired outcomes, students' proficiency levels, materials needed to carry out lesson, duration of the lesson, and highlighted strategies that can facilitate ELs' learning. Lessons in each chapter also follow a similar format and include procedures (the specific details regarding what the students will do during the lesson) and assessment and evaluation of the lesson. Finally, each chapter closes with a reflection that summarizes how the original TESOL research informs teachers' practice and raises valuable questions for further inquiry.

This series of books can be utilized by a wide range of participants in the TESOL community, including English language teachers, mainstream content-area teachers who work with ELs, program administrators, coaches, and trainers. Because of their teacher-friendly format and ancillary online resources, the books are appropriate for use as course readings for preservice and in-service teacher education programs and as professional development for teachers of ELs. Also, because the classroom contexts are set in schools throughout the United States, readers gain a breadth of understanding regarding standards, demographics, grade levels, and English as a second language programs.

In this volume, lessons are focused on the high school context, with student activities appropriate for ninth through twelfth grades. The chapters center on English language arts, social studies, science, and mathematics and address concepts such as guided visualization, argumentation, genre pedagogy, translanguaging, accountable talk, and use of graphic organizers and picture books. The research covered in this volume is cutting edge, insightful, and applicable to a broad range of ELT contexts at high school levels.

The contributors to the middle school volume represent a mix of teacher educators/researchers, undergraduate and graduate students, and middle school teachers, and many chapters are written in collaboration with various constituents. In this way, the chapters truly put research into practice in a clear, hands-on, accessible, and digestible way. It is my hope that you will benefit from—and enjoy—this compilation as much as I do!

Holly Hansen-Thomas
Texas Woman's University

Reference

TESOL International Association. (2014, November). Research agenda 2014. Alexandria, VA: Author. Retrieved from http://www.tesol.org/docs/default-source /pdf/2014_tesol-research-agenda.pdf?sfvrsn=2

Introduction

Mandy Stewart and Holly Hansen-Thomas

This volume of the Engaging Research series highlights the important work of 23 teachers and researchers who are involved in high school classrooms with students in the dynamic process of English language acquisition. The classrooms must set the optimal learning environment for not only high school–level content learning, but also English language acquisition. The authors of these chapters illustrate how high school educators can apply up-to-date TESOL research to meet both of those criteria (content and language acquisition) while also affirming students' cultural knowledge, individual lived experiences, and full language abilities. Through the research they bring to life within their lessons, the authors show how high school English learners (ELs) can thrive in the academic classroom—despite many inherent challenges.

Challenges of Teaching High School ELs

Teaching ELs at the high school level is a complex task because of the great variety of these students' lived experiences (Menken, 2013). There are many factors contributing to the diversity of this group, including the amount of their previous formal schooling and its environment, time in the English-speaking country, literacy skills in their first or home language(s), lived experiences, and cultural diversity (Faltis & Coulter, 2008). Age can even be a factor, because students from other countries are often assigned a birth year that does not represent their actual age, possibly as a result of having been given refugee status (Sonnert & Holton, 2010; Stewart, 2017). Moreover, many high school students are placed in ninth grade regardless of their ages because they need to acquire a certain number of credits to graduate high school, meaning there is a wide range of age and maturity level in these classes (Cloud, Lakin, Leininger, & Maxwell, 2010).

This volume unpacks two of the factors that we believe can greatly affect the challenges of teaching in the high school classroom: students' English proficiency level and their previous educational experiences. One important factor to consider is the students' language proficiency, or English language development (ELD) levels, in all language domains: reading, writing, listening, and speaking. Within the EL label, students' ELD levels vary widely and can run the gamut from entering (Level 1) to reaching (Level 6; WIDA, 2014). For example, many high school classrooms have students who are newcomers to the country who have little to no English language knowledge or proficiency. These students are sometimes referred to as late arrivals, suggesting the limited amount of time they have to learn language and content needed for high school graduation. However, there are also students in high school classrooms labeled long-term ELs (L-TELs) who have received language support services for 7 or more years (Olsen, 2010). These students, some of whom have even been born in the United States, often possess native-like social language skills in English, yet still struggle with academic language. Although they use English in very advanced ways, illustrating their ruled-governed use of one or more languages, these L-TELs have not met the required academic state standards (determined by high-stakes standardized tests) to exit them from English-as-a-second-language services. Of course, there are students with both oral and academic ELD levels that fall throughout this vast continuum. Thus, high school teachers have a herculean task: They must provide effective language support for students who have yet to produce a word in English; those who consider English their dominant language, yet still struggle academically; as well as the monolingual English speakers in their classes.

High school ELs' educational backgrounds play an important role in their success (or failure) in school. Many L-TELs will have had all or at least most of their formal schooling in the United States or an English-dominant country. If they still struggle academically, it is quite possible they have experienced subtractive schooling (Valenzuela, 1999), or a learning environment that continually devalued their language and cultural knowledge while also misunderstanding their linguistic identities (Brooks, 2017). Conversely, other students, particularly some newcomers, might have had years of excellent educational experiences in their home country where their language and culture were fully valued and they learned literacy and content knowledge to what the new country would consider age-appropriate levels. Yet other students are what are referred to as SIFES or SLIFES, students with interrupted formal education (Salva, 2017) or students with limited or interrupted formal education (Montero, Newmaster, & Ledger, 2014), respectively. These students have months, or even years, of gaps in their education because they could not attend a formal school due to circumstances such as war, migration, or extreme poverty. Conversely, some of these students might have consistently attended school, but they did not learn their first language or content knowledge to appropriate levels for reasons such as geographic, economic, wartime, or transnational/migratory conditions (Salva & Matis, 2017). Therefore, high school educators must understand the previous positive or negative educational experiences of their ELs as well as those critical lacunae students have experienced with regard to schooling. To best serve these learners, teachers need to know where their ELs attended school, what the conditions were, and how well developed their native language literacy is.

Additionally, there are external factors that greatly affect high school ELs' academic and social success. High school ELs in the United States are often children of immigrants, have at least one foreign-born parent, and have experienced triggers that have prompted their migration (Suárez-Orozco, Suárez-Orozco, & Todorova, 2008). Some of these students will have experienced various levels of trauma prior to coming to the high school classroom. In addition, older ELs might even be working many hours a week to support themselves and/or family or taking on other adult responsibilities in their lives. It is critical to understand and acknowledge such factors.

Promise and Potential

Whereas the challenges are often highlighted in the experience of immigrant students (Ruiz-de-Velasco, Fix, & Clewell, 2000), it is important to point out their promise and possibilities as well. Research shows that high school ELs will often possess transnational and multilingual skills that are very needed in our society, yet that are rare in monolingual nonimmigrant populations (Suárez-Orozco et al., 2008). High school ELs can contribute to their school, their communities, and our nation in unique and promising ways (Sadowski, 2013). In this volume, we acknowledge high school ELs' need to acquire high levels of both academic and social English skills while celebrating their culturally embedded knowledge, full linguistic repertoires, and unique perspectives. It is our desire that as you engage with research in the field of English language teaching, you will see how you can put that research into practice in your classroom to not only meet the challenges of teaching high school ELs, but to be able to see and build on their strengths.

Organization of the Book

The chapters in this volume are organized by the four primary content areas in high school in which students must demonstrate proficiency to graduate: English language arts, social studies, science, and mathematics. However, we maintain that the ideas and strategies presented by the contributing authors can be used across all content areas—including fine arts and world languages classrooms.

English Language Arts

In the first chapter, Misty Ferguson leverages the ever-present reality of high-stakes testing at the secondary level to illustrate an alternative approach to the skill of argumentation, which many teachers need to focus on for their students to achieve high school graduation and college entry. She illustrates how teachers can still deliver culturally relevant, creative, and engaging instruction to ELs while building a skill they need to master.

Next, Katie Walker takes into account her students' cultural knowledge when conducting her lesson on poetry. Focal learners are in a ninth-grade classroom, and many are Spanish-speaking ELs. In her classroom, Katie uses supports, such as graphic organizers and supplementary texts for building background knowledge, to guide students in their analysis and creation of poetry. This chapter also illustrates how the arts can support students' literacy and language development.

The final chapter in the English language arts section builds on the notion of translanguaging as an everyday classroom practice in a senior English classroom of Spanish/English bilinguals who are relatively new to the United States. Seth M. Ross and Mary Amanda Stewart illustrate how giving students opportunities and encouraging their use of all their languages in responding to literature can lead to greater higher order thinking, literacy development, and engagement with complex texts in English.

Social Studies

The three chapters in the social studies section have strong ties to the language arts, as they also use literature in their lessons. Jacqueline Riley and Patsy Sosa-Sánchez explain the benefits of the Sheltered Instruction Observation Protocol (SIOP; Echevarría, Vogt, & Short, 2008) model in the U.S. history classroom by teaching about migration from Mexico, specifically through using an adolescent novel as their focal text. The chapter authors explain the many SIOP strategies appropriate for using before, during, and after reading the novel that make both the history content and the academic language relevant and comprehensible to learners.

Using children's literature to teach history, Tamra Dollar, Patricia Flint, and Holly Hansen-Thomas share how they used a picture book to teach a group of newcomer ELs historical content from World War II, comprehension strategies of cause and effect, and vocabulary. Although picture books are most commonly thought of in the lower grades, the chapter authors use them in appropriate ways with older learners to help the newcomer students make meaning from text as they shift from the picture book to a historical article found online. The authors' experience teaching this lesson provides teachers with key strategies they can use to help their ELs comprehend complex texts often found in the social studies classroom.

Next, Laura Schall-Leckrone and Debbie Barron discuss genre pedagogy as a way to teach both language and content regarding the expansion of the Roman empire. The teacher in this lesson, the second author, provides the appropriate scaffolds to assist students in deconstructing and then constructing historical explanations. Through this engagement with history, students also develop more experience with complex linguistic features of history.

Science

The first chapter in the science section takes an overt multilingual stance to ESL or English to speakers of other languages teaching, acknowledging and leveraging the many first or home languages that ELs bring with them into the English-medium classroom. Brian Seilstad, Derek Braun, Somin Kim, and Min-Seok Choi share how high school ELs created biomes through The Bilingual Biome Project. Although the teacher did not speak all of the students' multiple home languages, he encouraged them to use all of their languages to work collaboratively, understand the vocabulary related to the project, and discuss the key concepts. The authors also illustrate how they honored students' cultural identities by encouraging them to select for the project a biome that exists in their countries of origin.

In the next chapter, Francine M. Johnson, Cynthia Lima, and Jorge Solís share a teaching exemplar in which they use a dialogic discourse strategy, accountable talk, to teach climate patterns. This lesson highlights the role of dialogue with peers in the science classroom to make sense of the content and further one's learning. The authors expertly illustrate how, when teaching ELs, the high school science teacher can attend both to language functions used in scientific practices and content knowledge.

Rounding out the section on science, Alandeom W. Oliveira, Luciana de Oliveira, and Carla Meskill discuss a lesson that teaches earthquake science through guided visualizations. They explain how teachers of ELs should carefully evaluate and plan how they will use visual aids to support student learning. By focusing on visual literacy throughout the lesson, ELs had appropriate scaffolding that allowed them to fully engage with the scientific content, leading to verbal practice and development. This chapter helps all teachers understand how to most effectively use a variety of visuals to enhance the language and content learning of their students.

Mathematics

The last chapter of the book focuses on math—specifically algebra, which happens to be a gatekeeping class for high schoolers. That is, algebra is a subject that most students must demonstrate proficiency or mastery in to graduate. Geraldine Devine and Suzanne Toohey introduce functional relationships and their representations through responsive and explicit language instruction within the math classroom. Specifically, the authors explain how the teachers purposefully incorporate reading, writing, speaking, and listening practice and scaffolding seamlessly throughout the algebra lesson to facilitate comprehension.

Overcoming the Challenges and Unveiling the Promise in the High School Classroom

These authors all acknowledge the challenges of teaching in the high school classroom with ELs, yet they all expertly illustrate the scaffolding that allows teachers to deliver dynamic language and content instruction simultaneously. They both tell and show how TESOL research can inform all content areas of the high school classroom. Most important, the lessons described in this volume also demonstrate the vast prior knowledge, unique geographic understandings, varied cultural practices, and multilingual linguistic abilities high school ELs possess. These abilities can be leveraged to maximize academic and social success. Surely, when students have the supports they need, when their strengths are leveraged, we will unveil the great promise ELs have in the high school classroom and beyond.

References

Brooks, M. (2017). How and when did you learn your languages? Bilingual students' linguistic experiences and literacy instruction. *Journal of Adolescent & Adult Literacy, 60*(4), 383–393.

Cloud, N., Lakin, J., Leininger, E., & Maxwell, L. (2010). *Teaching adolescent ELLs. Essential strategies for middle and high school.* Philadelphia, PA: Caslon.

Echevarría, J., Vogt, M., & Short, D. (2008). *Making content comprehensible for English learners: The SIOP model.* New York, NY: Pearson.

Faltis, C., & Coulter, C. (2008). *Teaching English learners and immigrant students in secondary schools.* Upper Saddle River, NJ: Pearson/Merrill Prentice Hall.

Menken, K. (2013). Emergent bilingual students in secondary school: Along the academic language and literacy continuum. *Language Teaching, 46*(4), 438–476.

Montero, K., Newmaster, S., & Ledger, S. (2014). Exploring early reading instructional strategies to advance the print literacy development of adolescent SLIFE. *Journal of Adolescent & Adult Literacy, 58*(1), 59–69. doi:10.1002/jaal.318.

Olsen, L. (2010). Reparable harm: Fulfilling the unkept promise of educational opportunity for California's long term English learners. Long Beach, CA: Californians Together.

Ruiz-de-Velasco, J., Fix, M., & Clewell, B. C. (2000). *Overlooked & underserved: Immigrant students in U.S. secondary schools.* The Urban Institute Report. Washington, DC: The Urban Institute.

Sadowski, M. (2013). *Portraits of promise: Voices of successful immigrant students.* Cambridge, MA: Harvard Education Press.

Salva, C., & Matis, A. (2017). *Boosting achievement: Reaching students with interrupted or minimal education.* Irving, TX: Seidlitz Education.

Sonnert, G., & Holton, G. J. (2010). *Helping young refugees and immigrants succeed: Public policy, aid, and education* (1st ed.). New York, NY: Palgrave Macmillan.

Stewart, M. A. (2017). "I love this book because that's like me!" A multilingual refugee/adolescent girl responds from her homeplace. *International Multilingual Research Journal, 11*(4), 239–254.

Suárez-Orozco, C., Suárez-Orozco, M. M., & Todorova, I. (2008). *Learning a new land: Immigrant students in American society.* Cambridge, MA: Belknap Press of Harvard University Press.

Valenzuela, A. (1999). *Subtractive schooling: U.S.-Mexican youth and the politics of caring.* Albany, NY: State University of New York Press.

World Class Instructional and Design and Assessment (WIDA). (2014). 2012 amplification of the English Language Development Standards: Kindergarten–grade 12.

Section 1

Language Arts

Approaching Argumentation Playfully in the English Language Arts Classroom

Misty Ferguson

Introduction

In the lesson presented in this chapter, teachers guide students in developing the skill of argumentation, which prepares students for success on both their state standardized assessments and their college gatekeeping exams. Additionally, the content and organization of the lesson encourages teachers to maintain evidenced-based best practices in their instruction even as they engage in preparing students for their examinations (Slavin, 2008). The lesson draws on Giouroukakis and Honigsfeld's (2010) research, published in *TESOL Journal*, in which they report ways that teachers deliver highly engaging, culturally relevant instruction that simultaneously functions as effective preparation for necessary examinations.

Standardized testing has been the preeminent mechanism for school reform in the United States since the imposition of No Child Left Behind (NCLB) as law in 2001 (Au & Hollar, 2016; Malsbary, 2016). These unfair and arguably invalid instruments wield outsized influence over instructional decisions from the level of state departments of education down to classrooms (Reyes & Villarreal, 2016). It is not an exaggeration to say that teachers typically hold standardized testing in disdain and are loath to engage in test preparation. In fact, many probably relate to this statement about standardized testing, made by one of the participating teachers in Giouroukakis and Honigsfeld's (2010) study: "It just sucks up all the oxygen in the room" (p. 487). Unfortunately, teaching to the test feels nearly unavoidable, especially in schools and classrooms serving English learners (ELs), regardless of how uncomfortable teachers may feel about allowing tests with dubious levels of validity for diverse learners to drive instructional decisions (Menken, 2006). However, as graduation is increasingly tied to test performance, teachers find themselves in a double bind, caught between their desire to pursue innovative and culturally responsive teaching and their awareness that the tests hold power over the trajectories of students' lives.

This lesson, which covers a unit plan, offers a way out of that bind through a playful approach to the skill of argumentation. By creatively approaching instruction for this ubiquitously tested skill, teachers are able to implement culturally relevant practices which are supported by research while helping students build the linguistic and rhetorical skills necessary for success on their standardized tests. This approach is accomplished primarily through a shift in materials and topic selection. Rather than bombarding students with the standard materials (e.g., released tests), in this unit, teachers present the skill set necessary for composing a logical argument through debatable topics that invite laughter and connection.

Synopsis of Original Research

Giouroukakis, V., & Honigsfeld, A. (2010). High-stakes testing and English language learners: Using culturally and linguistically responsive literacy practices in the high school English classroom. *TESOL Journal*, *1*, 470–499. doi:10.5054/tj.2010.240193

The testing culture in U.S. schools is all but impenetrable (Reyes & Villarreal, 2016). Researchers have established the harm testing has inflicted on teaching and learning, and no group seems more negatively affected than ELs (Bahruth, 2000; Bartolomé, 1994; de la Luz Reyes, 1992; del Carmen Salazar, 2013; Franquiz & del Carmen Salazar, 2004; Giroux, 2010; Huerta, 2011; Nichols & Berliner, 2007). Since NCLB became law, ELs' scores have not changed, nor has the so-called achievement gap closed significantly (Menken, 2008; Olson, Matuchniak, Chung, Stumpf, & Farkas, 2017). The literature detailing the negative effects of testing on ELs has yet to shift policy; thus, Enright (2010) argues that researchers would do well to embrace efforts aimed at "finding niches and practices" where teaching and learning within the current context can be optimized (p. 805). Giouroukakis and Honigsfeld's (2010) study illustrates that teachers have managed to maintain and embrace practices designed to foster authentic, meaningful learning while preparing ELs for particular assessments. Though condemning the current test-centric climate in U.S. schools, the four English and ESL teachers in the study designed instruction that afforded both test preparation and authentic learning. They accomplished this in large part by selecting materials inflected with the cultural and linguistic background of their students in spite of the overwhelming presence of the state tests as the driver of curricular decisions.

The impetus for Giouroukakis and Honigsfeld's (2010) research was Menken's (2006) article, in which she reported on the ways that standardized testing was shaping language policy in education from the classroom to the highest political platform. Though Menken's (2006) work focused primarily on urban schooling, Giouroukakis and Honigsfeld's work indicates similar results in suburban communities where the EL population is perhaps smaller but nonetheless significant. Their aim was to document how teachers, in spite of the pressures and power of the test, "challenge themselves to offer both pedagogically appropriate and culturally and linguistically responsive instruction while . . . teaching to the test to various degrees" (p. 489).

The design of their study included classroom observation and interviews of four teachers with English or English to Speakers of Other Languages (ESOL) certificates or both. All four teachers taught in public high schools in Long Island, New York, USA; all were tenth-grade teachers whose students were tested by the New York Regents exam, which students must pass to earn a New York state diploma. Thus, curriculum in their classes was explicitly designed to prepare students for this specific test. Over a 5-month period, Giouroukakis and Honigsfeld (2010) observed at least three lessons per teacher and interviewed each teacher three times. They also collected instructional documents from the teachers and had them respond to an online survey designed to elicit their personal teaching philosophy. These data were used to answer three research questions probing (1) the literacy tasks the teachers implemented in their classes and the degree to which those tasks were connected to the exam, (2) the type of test preparation materials the teachers used in their classes, and (3) the effects of the high-stakes exam on the teachers' beliefs about high-stakes testing and about their EL students.

Giouroukakis and Honigsfeld (2010) found that all four teachers acknowledged teaching to the test and observed them delivering instruction that focused on tested content and skills, including presenting specific test items and explicitly teaching test-taking strategies. Teachers admitted that certain parts of the school year were dominated by test preparation and that the content and pacing of their classes were fundamentally driven by the high-stakes Regents exam. Through interviews and observations, Giouroukakis and Honigsfeld were able to identify specific "test-preparation practices" their focal teachers enacted, including test-vocabulary instruction; analysis of and practice with released test questions; explanation of test rubrics; instruction on test-taking strategies; and intentional confidence-building activities connected to students' "test-taking self-concept," which one focal teacher considered the most challenging test-preparation practice to teach (p. 481).

However, even as teachers bemoaned the power of the exam over their instructional practices, they discussed their efforts to construct lessons built on culturally and linguistically sensitive pedagogy aimed toward authentic learning. Classroom observations confirmed that the four teachers did, in fact, systematically implement pedagogical practices (e.g., scaffolding and modeling) accompanied by various language accommodation strategies (e.g., sentence frames and graphic organizers). They also drew on culturally relevant teaching practices by including students' funds of knowledge (González, Moll, & Amanti, 2005), encouraging the use of students' first languages in the classroom and drawing from culturally responsive literature. Though the teachers did use released exam materials to encourage "test-savviness," they often adapted and augmented these materials with teacher-created materials designed to render test tasks more comprehensible and engaging to ELs. The teachers used authentic materials, drama and music, creative writing, and film to generate engagement with culturally relevant literature. These materials, which honored ELs' unique cultures and communities, facilitated connections between school tasks and the real world.

Teachers' careful reflection on the test's power in their students' lives coupled with deep concern for their students' unique needs drove efforts to prepare students for the powerful exam without abandoning the teachers' fundamental beliefs about grounding student learning in culturally and linguistically appropriate instruction and materials. These teachers were able to develop and deliver test preparation addressed through culturally responsive materials and tasks by implementing a purposeful instructional approach, nurturing a supportive learning environment, and providing meaningful instruction and materials aligned with research-based best practices for their diverse learners.

Based on their observations of and interactions with their four focal teachers, Giouroukakis and Honigsfeld (2010) posited that, in the current educational climate in the United States, teaching almost inevitably involves varying measures of test preparation. However, they stress that culturally and linguistically responsive high-stakes test preparation is possible when teachers integrate culturally appropriate literacy tasks and materials. This reflective, intentional teaching practice builds responsiveness into the pedagogy that can facilitate students' success on the test and engagement in learning through high-interest, culturally connected texts; performance-based products with written and oral components; and creative instruction designed to guide students' reading comprehension and nurture their voices. Further, they recommend teachers support students' linguistic development as they help them become test-smart through test-vocabulary development and analysis of test instructions and questions. This practice is enhanced when teachers embrace well-established practices, such as wait time, differentiated instruction, first language use, and peer interaction as part of a nurturing classroom culture built on encouragement and respect.

Rationale

Giouroukakis and Honigsfeld's (2010) study suggests that, though test preparation may alter good teaching, it does not negate it. They demonstrate that highly engaging, culturally relevant instruction does not have to fall by the wayside, victim of the hegemony of the test. In fact, in light of testing, creative approaches to literacy teaching and tasks are perhaps more vital than ever before.

The argumentation unit presented in this chapter explores one such creative approach. Here, teachers are invited to implement playful pedagogy in spite of the quite serious tests their students face, acknowledging that laughter and joy are central components of the particular set of cultural, linguistic, and social factors that make up students' profile (Fine, 2014; Herrera, Perez, & Escamilla, 2015). Research has shown that a playful approach enhances learners' self-esteem, affords authentic learning, builds community, and affords language acquisition (Conklin, 2014; Patte, 2012; Silver, 2010). Teaching is playful when it draws on the joy of learning, which lives at the core of human development across the lifespan (Göncü & Perone, 2005; Sutton-Smith, 1997). Playful teaching involves the intentional selection and presentation of content, assignments, and structure and the delivery of materials in imaginative, open-ended, and active ways.

This approach to teaching has deep, though often overlooked, empirical support. Sawyer (2015), for example, echoed Csikszentmihalyi (1990) when he claimed that happiness and well-being are linked specifically to participating in creative classroom activities. Chang, Hsu, and Chen (2013) found that playful classroom environments resulted in increased student creativity. He, Prater, and Steed (2011) pointed out that effectively teaching ELs involves not only a knowledge of language domains but also requires an understanding of how to connect across cultures and that playfulness offers an avenue through which to forge such a connection. Silver (1999) intentionally added play to his students' daily agenda and found that, when he did, ELs both developed their English skills and created deeper connections to their classmates.

This lesson, then, seeks to present a way to teach argumentation through joy and creativity. In terms of Giouroukakis and Honigsfeld's (2010) recommendations, this lesson values students' out-of-school experiences, culturally embedded ways of knowing, and knowledge of pop culture. The tasks generate performance-based products of learning that spring from a creative experience with building and writing arguments. Giouroukakis and Honigsfeld (2010) also recommend linguistically responsive practices, which are represented in this unit as well: Students are presented with step-by-step instruction, plenty of peer interaction, essay and sentence frames, oral practice before writing, and interpersonal support via teamwork and coaching.

Lesson Plan

Lesson Plan Title	Playing With Arguments
Grade/Subject Area	Grades 9–12 ; English language arts, English as a second language
Duration	≈ 2 weeks
Proficiency Levels	WIDA (2007): Levels 2–5 (Beginning to Bridging)
Content and Language Objectives	Students will be able to • define and differentiate fact, opinion, and logic as they apply themselves to developing arguments by surveying and conversing with their classmates on a position and organizing their responses. (Content) • orally state their reasons for taking a position and support those reasons with examples, logic, or fact by participating in paired and group debates. (Content) • write an argumentative essay stating a clear position and providing reasons along with examples, logic, and fact as support by using essay, paragraph, and sentence frames. (Content) • use the terms *argument, argumentation, fact, opinion,* and *logic* accurately in a class discussion as they complete a graphic organizer labeling their peers' responses to "Would You Rather" questions. (Language) • participate in paired and small group debates in which they will take a position and support that position with fact and logic by using sentence frames. (Language) • write an argumentative essay (both with a group and individually) in which they take a position and support that position through logic and fact by using essay, paragraph, and sentence frames. (Language)

(continued on next page)

Lesson Plan *(continued)*	
Alignment to Standards	**Common Core State Standards** (NGA & CCSSO, 2010) Standards for argumentative writing; listening comprehension and collaboration; problem-solving through research, logic, and cooperation; presentations of reasonable arguments; and source evaluation. For example: • *CCSS.ELA-LITERACY.W.9-10.1*: Write arguments to support claims in an analysis of substantive topics or texts, using valid reasoning and relevant and sufficient evidence. • *CCSS.ELA-LITERACY.SL.9-10.1*: Initiate and participate effectively in a range of collaborative discussions (one-on-one, in groups, and teacher-led) with diverse partners on grades 9–10 topics, texts, and issues, building on others' ideas and expressing their own clearly and persuasively. • *CCSS.ELA-LITERACY.SL.11-12.1*: Initiate and participate effectively in a range of collaborative discussions (one-on-one, in groups, and teacher-led) with diverse partners on grades 11–12 topics, texts, and issues, building on others' ideas and expressing their own clearly and persuasively. • *CCSS.ELA-LITERACY.SL.11-12.2*: Integrate multiple sources of information presented in diverse formats and media (e.g., visually, quantitatively, orally) in order to make informed decisions and solve problems, evaluating the credibility and accuracy of each source and noting any discrepancies among the data. • *CCSS.ELA-LITERACY.SL.9-10.4*: Present information, findings, and supporting evidence clearly, concisely, and logically such that listeners can follow the line of reasoning and the organization, development, substance, and style are appropriate to purpose, audience, and task. • *CCSS.ELA-LITERACY.SL.11-12.4*: Present information, findings, and supporting evidence, conveying a clear and distinct perspective, such that listeners can follow the line of reasoning, alternative or opposing perspectives are addressed, and the organization, development, substance, and style are appropriate to purpose, audience, and a range of formal and informal tasks. • *CCSS.ELA-LITERACY.SL.9-10.3*: Evaluate a speaker's point of view, reasoning, and use of evidence and rhetoric, identifying any fallacious reasoning or exaggerated or distorted evidence. • *CCSS.ELA-LITERACY.SL.11-12.3*: Evaluate a speaker's point of view, reasoning, and use of evidence and rhetoric, assessing the stance, premises, links among ideas, word choice, points of emphasis, and tone used.

Lesson Plan *(continued)*	
Outcomes	Students will • participate in a debate and write both a group and an individual argumentative essay with at least three points of argument and one of counter argument. • internalize the basic elements of a quality argument and of writing an argumentative essay, which will serve them both as they craft timed essays in testing situations and as they build on these foundational skills toward more sophisticated persuasive essays.
Materials	• Overhead projector or document camera • Appendixes A–D (available on the companion website for this book): — Which Would You Rather handout (Appendix A) — Questions for Speed Debate handout (Appendix B) — The Argument Builder handout (Appendix C) — Handouts of essay frames (Appendix D) — Sentence stems for posting (Appendix E) — Timed Essay: Steps to Essay Writing worksheet (Appendix F) • Copies of Frank Stockton's (1882) short story "Lady or the Tiger?" for each student

This lesson plan was developed for Grade 11 students who were being prepared for success not only on their state's standardized assessment but also on college-entrance exams (e.g., the SAT). Designed to support students who are developing their English language skills as well as those whose academic background may have some gaps, the materials were presented with language support, yet students at higher levels of English development or with more experience in writing argumentative essays may need fewer scaffolds.

Highlighted Teaching Strategies

This lesson utilized the following teaching strategies:

• Thematic question: "How can you change someone's mind?"

• Oral argumentation around low-risk, silly questions that nonetheless demand the production of logical, fact-based arguments

• Sentence stems

• Paragraph and essay frames

• Peer interaction

Procedures

Day 1

For warm-up, have students pick up the Which Would You Rather handout (Appendix A) as they walk in the room. Once seated, they follow the instructions on the handout, selecting one answer only to the "Would you rather . . . ?" questions presented. Allow them a few minutes to complete their answers.

Call the group to attention, and, using a copy of the handout projected on the overhead projector or document camera, take a survey of the students' responses. For example, you might ask, "Who said they'd rather not use their phone for a month? Who'd rather eat bread and drink water for a month if you still had your phone?"

Write down the number of responses to each position offered by the question. Create a table with the questions and answers for and against clearly marked. Ask a few students who respond, "Why did you choose that?" Allow whole-class discussion among the students as they offer one another support and/or disagree. Debate is sure to break out!

Explain to the students that they have (1) taken a position and (2) supported their chosen positions by creating arguments. Have them think about how they are forming their arguments. Ask them to consider the basis of their arguments. Elicit the terms *opinion*, *facts*, *emotion* (*feelings*), *logic*, and *reasons*. Write the terms on the board, having students record them in their notebooks or vocabulary lists if keeping them are routine in your classes.

Together with the students, write definitions for the terms. Ask students to help you rank which elements create the most convincing arguments and explain their selections. You can use YouTube videos to help students understand these concepts. For example videos and questions, see the companion website for this book.

Return to the table you created showing positions and explanations. Label each explanation as fact, reason, emotion, opinion, and so on.

For homework, have students ask friends or family members two or three "Would you rather . . . ?" questions from the handout. They may write down the answers or video- or audio-record themselves asking them, and then they should write or record their analysis considering how their interviewees supported their positions.

Day 2

The main activity of Day 2 is a "speed debate." This works best if students are able to stand or be seated facing one another. They will need to shift positions (one line move to the right, one to the left) in order that pairs change for each question. Depending on the space in your room or the way it is furnished, you may be able to line up the desks facing one another, having students configure themselves as shown in the video, "Inside/Outside Circles" (www.theteachertoolkit.com/index .php/tool/inside-outside-circles), from TheTeacherToolkit.com. Print the Speed Debate Questions (Appendix B). You will need two copies of each question, one for each facing desk. The cards should be exactly the same, but you should circle opposing answers. For example, both cards will say, "Which would be easier to take care of: a pet dragon or a pet blue whale?"; on one card, circle "dragon" and, on the other, circle "blue whale." This will be the position the students will take in paired debate. Place cards on facing desks. Students will move, but the cards will remain on the desks. This will allow for students to pair with new partners and to debate new questions with each turn.

Seat students in the facing desks and have them show one another portions of the videos they recorded last night for homework. Then, ask them two more "Would You Rather" questions. As soon as they answer, have their speaking partner ask, "Why?" and agree or disagree, providing their own reasons. Here are some ideas for questions:

- Would you rather have three hands or three legs? (See the Huffington Post article on the companion website for this book.)
- Would you rather always be 20 minutes late or always be 10 minutes early?
- Would you rather lose your money or all of the pictures you have ever taken?
- Would you rather be able to see 10 years into your own future or someone else's?

Briefly review the terms introduced in the last class (*argument, argumentation, opinion, facts, emotion, logic, reasons,* etc.). Add the term *counter-argument* with its definition: "A counter-argument is someone's reason to oppose an idea or to see the logic in a different way." Explain that today students will be engaged in a "speed debate" with their classmates in which they will defend a position through argument and counter-argument.

Give students the following instructions:

> At each desk, you'll find a card with a question and a preselected position. You will have 2 minutes to read the question, consider the position, and develop two or three reasons that the position selected on your card is the better choice of the two. You'll need notebooks and pens or pencils to write down a few notes. Then, one of you will have 2 minutes to argue your position to your partner. Next, your partner, with the opposing position, will have a chance to deliver their argument for 2 minutes. Finally, each of you will be given 1 additional minute to explain to your partner what is missing from their argument and to reinforce why your own position is the better one.

This final minute often gets entertainingly animated. If you are not comfortable with elevated volume in the classroom, go over some ground rules before beginning the debates.

Post and go over the following sentence stems for arguing for and against positions:

- I think that X is the better choice because . . .
- One reason that X is a better choice is that . . .
- I argue that X is the better choice because . . .
- You're ignoring the fact that . . .
- Your argument isn't logical because . . .

- You may be right about X, but you're not considering Y because . . .
- I find your explanation/evidence/reasoning/logic weak because . . .

Have two students come to the front of the class and perform one speed debate with you as a model. Appoint another student the timer. Model the debate process, supporting your student partner by cueing the sentence stems and helping them to develop arguments and counter-arguments. If necessary, repeat the process or have a pair of students model a debate in front of the class.

Begin the debate, having students shift seats (one side moves left, one side moves right in order that students are paired with every other student) at the end of each 5-minute session. At the end of each session, playfully ask students, "Who won?"

At the end of class, discuss what about arguing was easy or hard. Ask whether anyone felt convinced by their debate partner's arguments or counter-arguments.

Assign the following for homework:

> Write a paragraph (or entry on the class blog or on another online resource, such as Padlet or Edmodo) stating what you think was your best argument today. What did you say that really made sense?

Days 3–4

For warm-up, have students discuss what they wrote for last night's homework. Tell them to explain to someone who has not yet heard their argument. Challenge the new listener to come up with a counter-argument that might make the original arguer change positions. Have a few people share with the class.

Explain that today, students will prepare arguments for a group debate. Present the debate format and new sentence stems for oral debate. Depending on your class size, you may have four groups of two or three students and hold two debates on the same topic simultaneously or simply hold one debate after another on distinct topics and have the other groups serve as judges. Your decision will depend in part on the space and time available. Alternatively, this activity can be extended, allowing students to debate two different topics to build and practice their skills.

Define necessary terms (initial argument, rebuttal, concluding remarks) and explain to students that the debate format will be:

- Initial argument: 2 minutes each
- Follow-up argument: 2 minutes each
- Rebuttal: 2 minutes each
- Concluding remarks: 1 minute each

Decide together as a class the judging criterion. Ask students, "What makes a strong argument?" and "What sort of argument should earn points/lose points?" Sketch out a system for awarding points on the board or document camera.

Explain that each group will have the rest of today's class to develop their arguments and prepare their remarks. Offer the follow paragraph frames:

- We strongly believe X for three reasons. The first/second/third reason is . . .
- Our position is that . . .

- When you argue that X, you neglect the fact that . . .
- We concede that X is maybe true, but your argument ignores . . .
- Our opponents have argued that X . . . but our view is that a more logical conclusion is Y because . . .

Present students with the following debate topics.

- *Debate 1: The superhero that the worlds needs now is _____.*
- Fact in this debate comes from superhero movies, comic books, and books. Students may nominate specific heroes and then limit their selection to two opposing options.
- *Debate 2: Which are fiercer: unicorns or house cats?*

  Fact in this debate comes from books, movies, and folklore.
- *Debate 3: Which would create a better future: a machine that would wrap every car and plane in an impenetrable cloud of safety or a machine that would slap anyone who tried to say something mean?*

  The quality of logical connections to facts about the real world will determine the winner of this debate.
- *Debate 4: Who would make a better friend: Minnie Mouse or Pikachu?*

  Characters for this debate could be nominated by students or could reflect literature that students have read in class or studied in social studies (e.g., Jay Gatsby vs. Tom Sawyer, Abraham Lincoln vs. Wild Bill Hickok). Fact in this debate comes from books and film—the characters' stories, whether fictional or factual.

Assign students to groups based on the debate topic they select. These are just a few selections. It is always an interesting approach to have students formulate the debate topics and to determine what counts as fact. They do however, often need guidance to see that arguments of pure opinion (e.g., Which tastes better: Coke or Pepsi?) are not topics that can be conceptualized logically because any argument would be based purely on personal preferences—this discussion in itself is a vitally important one. Topics of local interest also work well, though be cautious in choosing debates that may be too emotionally charged or too connected to some students' personal identities (e.g., sports teams, sides of town, gender) because this can jeopardize the spirit of fun and discovery. It is key that topics are light and novel or at least framed in a novel way. (E.g., We are about to colonize Mars: Should people in the settlements be allowed to own property or should all property be owned collectivity?)

Assign the following for homework:

> Write or video record a report of what you think was the best debate of the day. Explain your choice and comment on your experience of debating or listening. Did you change your mind based on the arguments made by any team? Why or why not? Post your paragraph or your video on the [class blog/Facebook page/Padlet/Edmodo] or bring in a written copy.

Day 5

As students come in, they encounter a question posted on the board with instructions to write down their initial answer along with the reasons for their choice. The question should be something that demands a choice based on a certain criterion (e.g., Which would make a person happier: unlimited love or unlimited money?)

Explain that today's assignment will be to write argumentative essays in groups. Introduce or review the terms *thesis statement*, *reasons*, *evidence/support*, *counter-argument*, and *rebuttal*. Explain that, step-by-step, you will lead the class in developing an essay outline. On the overhead or document projector, follow The Argument Builder handout (Appendix C), constructing an outline based on the position the students select and the reasons, support, evidence, and counter-arguments they provide.

Assign groups of three students and offer them new questions or questions they have already encountered in the debates (students who are at earlier levels of English development will benefit from maintaining the same question they defended in the debate). Allow time for the group to read the question, select a position, and begin to develop their support. They should use the Argument Builder to create their outline.

For homework, groups should divide the paragraphs of the essay, and each member should bring in a first draft of their assigned paragraph.

Day 6

Have students reassemble in their groups and read through the drafts each brought as homework.

Present the essay frame and corresponding sentence stems (Appendixes D and E). The essay frame should broadly cover what the function of each paragraph/section should accomplish and provide some guidance for wording.

Model by providing examples of how this frame and these stems would be used: Compose portions of text on the overhead projector or document camera using the outline the students created in concert during Day 5. It is also a good idea to post frames and stems in the classroom:

- Introduction: Create interest, explain the importance of the issue, and establish any background necessary to understand the selected position.

- Thesis statement: Reword the question including your reasons.

  (<u>Your choice of positions</u>) would make a person happier than (<u>the other position</u>) because (<u>briefly state reasons one, two, and three</u>).

- Body paragraphs: Present reasons and well-connected evidence; place counter-arguments in paragraphs where they fit.

  The first reason that _____ would make someone happier is that _____. [Explain why this reason makes sense.]

  Some may argue that _____, but they are ignoring

  _____.

- Conclusion: Restate thesis and answer the question, "Why should the reader care?"

> A clear consideration of the evidence indicates that (restate your thesis).
>
> Understanding that _____ is vitally important, because _____ .

Allow time for student groups to compose their essays, revising the drafts they brought as homework in light of the frame and stems provided. Assign the following for homework:

> In an email to your teacher, reflect on your essay writing in groups today. Write about what is easy and hard about creating an argumentative essay. What questions do you still have?

Day 7

Prepare essay tests that align with the style of questioning and formatting of the argumentative essay question in the test your students are facing. Use another silly question in the style students have been writing to mimic the testing situation. Leave all classroom posters and notes up and available for student use. Appendix F offers a timed-essay form that provides further support as students internalize both the essay-writing process and the features of argumentation.

Discuss briefly with students any strengths and weaknesses you observed in their group essays written during Day 6. Explain that today's assignment will follow the same process but will be completed individually and within a specific time frame.

Pass out the question and remind students both what their thinking process should be (this was visualized on The Argument Builder handout) and what to write (this has been practiced through the essay frames and supported by posted sentence stems). Give students an appropriate amount of class time to write their timed essays.

Day 8

For warm-up, have students pick up a handout of the short story, "The Lady or the Tiger?" by Frank Stockton (1882). Links to the story can be found on the companion website for this book; there is a link to an unabridged version and, for students who may need a recorded, reduced, or guided version of the text, a Voice of America version.

Explain that, today, groups will read a story that will ask them their final argumentative question for the unit. Allow students to choose their favorite way to read—whether alone, listening to a read-aloud, or reading in a group. Organize the various types of readers into groups and allow them to read, instructing them to debate the question the story asks in their groups.

Once all groups have finished reading and are in the midst of debate, explain that their final essay, an individual argumentative essay, will answer the question posed by the story. Depending on how your students respond to the story, you may allow them to determine a third way that the story could end—neither the lady nor the tiger but a conclusion that they develop themselves and support from the text. In this

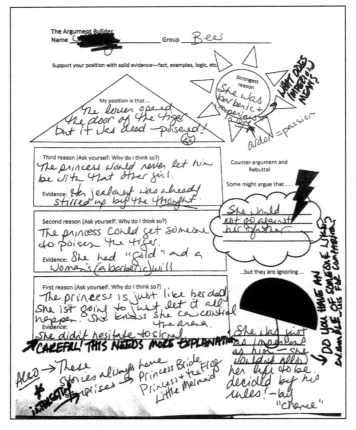

Figure 1. Student sample of Argument Builder handout
showing alternate ending option, with teacher annotation.

case, they must logically argue why neither the lady nor the tiger would be a logical conclusion and explain a plausible third way the story could end. You could develop a specific essay frame for this answer format if students require the support.

Distribute another round of Argument Builder handouts and allow students to begin to form their opinions. Explain that logic (i.e., appeals to what we know about human relationships and human nature) and the text itself will serve as sources of evidence.

For homework, have students complete the Argument Builder handout.

Days 9–10

Days 9 and 10 are writing workshops. In a writing workshop, you act as a mentor as students move through their writing process. Students may need assistance from you and peers as they work to construct their argument and to defend it through logical reasoning. You may pair students who have opposing positions to help them generate arguments and to develop their thinking through speaking. Additionally, you may present mini-lessons addressing areas in which students appear to need support.

Closing

You may wish to hold a final debate in which students defend their "Lady or the Tiger?" positions, or you may want to publish the essay after students have a chance to read your comments and revise. In any case, students are often eager to talk about their answers and enjoy debating the story's ending.

Extensions

If your school has a debate club or team, it would be a great time to schedule students from the team or the team's sponsor to present their club/team to your students. Evidence indicates that ELs or those who struggle with standardized tests often are not given adequate exposure to extra-curricular activities, even though participation in extracurricular opportunities has been connected to academic achievement and socioemotional well-being in ELs (Oikonomidoy, 2009; Páez, 2009).

Caveats

You may want to make argumentation more connected to sources. This lesson can be easily modified toward that purpose without sacrificing the element of fun connected to the use of silly topics. A question like, "Which would make a better president: a beaver or an otter?" requires source work as students discover (1) what it takes to be a good president and (2) the characteristics of both beavers and otters that might lend themselves to an effective presidency. This approach maintains the light-hearted spirit of the lesson along with its power to avoid plagiarism and push genuine logical thinking.

Assessment and Evaluation

Student assessment is both formative and summative in this unit. You are able to provide real-time feedback through the speed debate and the group debates. Students turn in their Argument Builders, their group essays, their timed essays, and then, of course, their final essay for evaluation and feedback.

Reflection on and Analysis of the Lesson

Before creating this unit, I used to dread teaching the argumentative essay. I was constantly frustrated because student papers would be either awash with plagiarism or dead-ended by students' sincerely held but poorly defended opinions. Classroom discussions were characterized by a few vocal students sounding off, while others took offence or shrunk from the conflict. The playful lesson outlined here, on the other hand, incites laughter, good-natured banter, and conversations that linger out the door and down the hallway. Groups giggle as they develop logical arguments that three legs would be more beneficial to the average person than three arms. Students come back in the next day eager to continue, having finally figured out the best way to defend their position. Because no one is emotionally invested in the answers, students cocreate fresh, vibrant arguments from the ground up. Students learn to process information in the way they will need, in the future, to question assumptions they may or may not be developmentally or linguistically ready to encounter at the moment. The thinking skills will be there, though, when they are ready.

The appendixes and additional resources for this chapter are available at www.tesol.org/practices-highschool.

Misty Ferguson is a doctoral candidate at the University of Texas at San Antonio, USA, where she studies the possibilities of playful learning and teaching for culturally and linguistically diverse students.

References

Au, W., & Hollar, J. (2016). Opting out of the education reform industry. *Monthly Review, 67*(10), 29–37.

Bahruth, R. E. (2000). Changes and challenges in teaching the word and the world for the benefit of all of humanity. In J. E. Katchen & L. Yiu-Nam (Eds.), *Selected papers from the Ninth International Symposium on English Teaching* (pp. 1–9). Taipei, Taiwan: Crane.

Bartolomé, L. (1994). Beyond the methods fetish: Toward a more humanizing pedagogy. *Harvard Educational Review, 64,* 173–195.

Chang, C. P., Hsu, C. T., & Chen, I. J. (2013). The relationship between the playfulness climate in the classroom and student creativity. *Quality & Quantity 47*(3), 1–18.

Conklin, H. G. (2014). Toward more joyful learning: Integrating play into frameworks of middle grades teaching. *American Educational Research Journal, 51*(6), 1227–1255.

Csikszentmihalyi, M. (1990). *Flow and the psychology of discovery and invention.* New York, NY: Harper Collins.

de la Luz Reyes, M. (1992). Challenging venerable assumptions: Literacy instruction for linguistically different students. *Harvard Educational Review, 62,* 427–446.

del Carmen Salazar, M. (2013). A humanizing pedagogy reinventing the principles and practice of education as a journey toward liberation. *Review of Research in Education, 37*(1), 121–148.

Enright, K. A. (2010). Academic literacies and adolescent learners: English for subject-matter secondary classrooms. *TESOL Quarterly, 44,* 804–810.

Fine, S. (2014). "A slow revolution": Toward a theory of intellectual playfulness in high school classrooms. *Harvard Educational Review, 84*(1), 1–23.

Franquiz, M. E., & del Carmen Salazar, M. (2004). The transformative potential of humanizing pedagogy: Addressing the diverse needs of Chicano/Mexicano students. *The High School Journal, 87*(4), 36–53.

Giouroukakis, V. & Honigsfeld, A. (2010). High-stakes testing and English language learners: Using culturally and linguistically responsive literacy practices in the high school English classroom. *TESOL Journal, 1,* 470–499. doi:10.5054/tj.2010.240193

Giroux, H. (2010, November 23). *Lessons to be learned from Paulo Freire as education is being taken over by the mega rich.* Retrieved from http://www.truth-out.org/archive /component/k2/item/93016:lessons-to-be-learned-from-paulo-freire-as-education -is-being-taken-over-by-the-mega-rich

Göncü, A., & Perone, A. (2005). Pretend play as a life-span activity. *Topoi, 24*(2), 137–147.

González, N., Moll, L. C., & Amanti, C. (Eds.). (2005). *Funds of knowledge.* London, England: Routledge.

He, Y., Prater, K., & Steed, T. (2011). Moving beyond 'just good teaching': ESL professional development for all teachers. *Professional Development in Education, 37*(1), 7–18.

Herrera, S. G., Perez, D. R., & Escamilla, K. (2015). *Teaching reading to English language learners: Differentiating literacies.* London, England: Pearson.

Huerta, T. M. (2011). Humanizing pedagogy: Beliefs and practices on the teaching of Latino children. *Bilingual Research Journal, 34*(1), 38–57.

Malsbary, C. B. (2016). The refusal: Teachers making policy in NYC. *International Journal of Qualitative Studies in Education, 29*(10), 1326–1338.

Menken, K. (2006). Teaching to the test: How No Child Left Behind impacts language policy, curriculum, and instruction for English language learners. *Bilingual Research Journal, 30*(2), 521–546.

Menken, K. (2008). *English learners left behind: Standardized testing as language policy.* Clevedon, England: Multilingual Matters.

National Governors Association Center for Best Practices and the Council of Chief State School Officers. (2010). Common Core State Standards for English language arts & literacy in history/social studies, science, and technical subjects. Washington, DC: Author.

Nichols, S. L., & Berliner, D. C. (2007). *Collateral damage: How high-stakes testing corrupts America's schools.* Cambridge, MA: Harvard Education Press.

Oikonomidoy, E. (2009). The multilayered character of newcomers' academic identities: Somali female high-school students in a US school. *Globalisation, Societies and Education, 7*(1), 23–39.

Olson, C. B., Matuchniak, T., Chung, H. Q., Stumpf, R., & Farkas, G. (2017). Reducing achievement gaps in academic writing for Latinos and English learners in grades 7–12. *Journal of Educational Psychology, 109*(1), 1–21.

Páez, M. (2009). Predictors of English-language proficiency among immigrant youth. *Bilingual Research Journal, 32*(2), 168–187.

Patte, M. (2012). Implementing a playful pedagogy in a standards-driven curriculum: Rationale for action research in teacher education. In L. Cohen & S. Waite-Stupiansky (Eds.) *Play: A polyphony of research, theories, and issues* (pp. 67–89). Lanham, MD: University Press of America.

Reyes, R., III, & Villarreal, E. (2016). Wanting the unwanted again: Safeguarding against normalizing dehumanization and discardability of marginalized, "unruly" English-learning Latinos in our schools. *The Urban Review, 48*(4), 543–559.

Sawyer, K. (2015). A Call to action: The challenges of creative teaching and learning. *Teachers College Record, 117*(10), 1–34.

Silver, A. (1999). Play: A fundamental equalizer for ESL children. *TESL Canada Journal, 16*(2), 62–69.

Slavin, R. E. (2008). Cooperative learning, success for all, and evidence-based reform in education. *Éducation et didactique, 2*(2), 149–157.

Stockton, F. R. (1882). The lady or the tiger? *The Century, 25*(1), 83–86.

Sutton-Smith, B. (1997). *The ambiguity of play.* Cambridge, MA: Harvard University Press.

World Class Instructional and Design and Assessment. (2007). English language proficiency standards grade 6 through grade 12. Retrieved from https://www.wida.us/standards/eld.aspx

El Cucuy and the Boogeyman: A Multicultural Arts-Based Approach to Poetry

Katie Walker

Introduction

Much of the current research on English as a second language (ESL) instruction has focused on the importance of leveraging students' home language and culture to promote lasting language and literacy learning. This research covers many topics related to leveraging students' knowledge from a variety of theoretical perspectives. One major issue is the idea that an effective educational environment provides a "third space" in which the discourses and cultures of school and community can merge (Moje et al., 2004), while another approach challenges educators to consider the way they define students that are learning English. García (2009) stated that using the term "emergent bilinguals" to refer to students who speak languages other than English increases equity for language minority students in education by openly acknowledging their bilingualism.

Though many educators that agree with the preceding general philosophies, they struggle with conceptualizing specific ways in which to apply these philosophies in their instruction. The lesson plan I present in this chapter focuses on specific strategies for leveraging students' home languages and cultures in a mainstream high school English language arts class. In this 2-week lesson, ninth-grade students engage in storytelling, photography, poetry analysis, poetry writing, and poetry performance. Students' home languages and cultures are threaded throughout the lesson by relying on oral stories that students bring from home (Perry, 2008), community-based art created by students (Friesen, 2012), and the use of first language (L1) and second language (L2) in student oracy and writing (Cahnmann-Taylor, Bleyle, Hwang, & Zhang, 2017).

Synopsis of Original Research

Cahnmann-Taylor, M., Bleyle, S., Hwang, Y., & Zhang, K. (2017). Teaching poetry in TESOL teacher education: Heightened attention to language as well as to cultural and political critique through poetry writing. *TESOL Journal, 8,* 70–101. doi:10.1002/tesj.263

In their 2017 study, Cahnmann-Taylor, Bleyle, Hwang, and Zhang offered poetry-writing courses as an optional elective for preservice TESOL educators. Over the course of three semesters, 38 native- and nonnative-English-speaking preservice TESOL teachers enrolled in the courses and participated in the study. During the courses, the preservice teachers engaged in (1) apprenticeship in poetic craft, (2) drafting poetry, (3) discourse in the format of writing workshops, and (4) poetry performance. The researchers found that embedding poetry in the TESOL education courses positively impacted the affective, linguistic, and academic domains of learning for both native and nonnative English speakers.

The researchers grounded the study in Pratt's (1991) concept of the "contact zone," which she defined as the "social spaces where cultures meet, clash, and grapple with each other, often in contexts of highly asymmetrical relations of power, such as colonialism, slavery, or their aftermaths as they are lived out in many parts of the world today" (p. 34). The contact zone is the physical, social, and cultural dynamics of the classroom, as well as the availability of textual space where students were situated, "literally and figuratively between languages, cultures, and world views" (p. 80).

Within this context, the researchers applied an arts-based approach to writing. In an arts-based approach to writing, the teacher pairs the writing with an aesthetic tool, such as a piece of music, art, or poetry. This approach was shaped by the ideas that combining writing with an aesthetic tool (Dabach, 2010)—language and play guided by elements of poetry (Moore, 2002)—and focusing on self-expression and creativity (Chappell & Faltis, 2013) effectively support the language and literacy development of English learners (ELs). The researchers believed that by providing students with an arts-based avenue to explore language, without the pressures of mastering standard English, students would be able to engage in authentic writing experiences that positioned the writer as an effective architect of language and self-expression.

According to Cahnmann-Taylor et al. (2017), the key findings of the research demonstrated that arts-based education, particularly poetry, provides opportunities for students to "celebrate the hybridized international and bilingual identities" (p. 83). The L2 preservice teachers in the study reported that poetry writing allowed room for them to maintain their true voice and identity while engaging in L2 writing. The researchers noticed that this approach appeared to reduce anxieties related to language correctness by encouraging students to focus on language play, expression, and the ability to convey meaning. Additionally, the L1 preservice teachers reported the experience provided them with insight into the cultures and abilities of their L2 peers. Many of the L1 preservice teachers assumed that their writing would be superior to that of their L2 peers, but they found that to be untrue. Instead, L1 preservice teachers reported that by the end of the study, they felt that the experience had leveled the playing field and that all preservice teachers in the class were seen as capable, creative producers of language. All of the students in the class, both L1 and L2, reported that having the opportunity to share their writing in a diverse classroom provided them with fresh ideas for style, form, content, and cultural understandings. Overall, the researchers concluded that the use of arts-based instruction occurring within the contact zone worked to create a democratized educational setting in which all students are skillful language producers.

Rationale

Though the authors of the article focused on using an arts-based approach within the contact zone with preservice TESOL teachers, there are direct connections to the body of research regarding effective practices for adolescent ELs. This chapter focuses on adapting the concepts and methods in Cahnmann-Taylor et al.'s (2017) study as a way to create a linguistic and cultural third space in which to analyze and create poetry within the high school English classroom. The lesson provided in this chapter draws on practices that connect the in- and out-of-school language, literacies, and cultures of adolescent native English speakers and ELs as a way to transition the concept of the contact zone to the idea of a cultural and linguistic third space for the purposes of this lesson. This is accomplished by asking students to begin their writing using stories that are frequently told in their families, such as family histories, folk tales, fables, myths, or any other story that has been passed down through oral tradition. During the writing process, students are asked to use language that reflects the language of their families as a poetic device. Providing all students with permission to embrace their whole identity in the classroom will hopefully allow high school students with a safe entrance into an educational setting in which they are required to deal with sensitive and conflicting issues of language, experiences, and cultures and also increase intrinsic motivation for engaging in the writing process.

In addition, students engage in discourse centered on their writings in the format of a writer's workshop. During these workshops, students share their poetry for the purpose of giving and receiving feedback. As in Cahnmann-Taylor et al.'s (2017) study, the workshops serve as opportunities for students to gain new insights and ideas for how they intend to construct their writing. The workshops not only provide support to students in their writing, but also support the creation of the third space in the classroom, so that native and nonnative English speakers can begin to share their understandings.

Finally, the lesson draws on the idea that poetry offers students an opportunity to improve their English language proficiency through apprenticeship and the functions of poetry that encourage self-expression, creativity, and language play. Students are assisted further through a common shared text, referred to as a touchstone text, that the class uses for poetry analysis, "Jabberwocky" (Carroll, 2001). By choosing a touchstone text that uses nonsense words, the various linguistic proficiencies in the class are equalized, because the focus is redirected from correctness to function and the ability to convey meaning. The poem is analyzed as a whole group, and the framework of the poem provides specific guidelines for poetry writing. The students mold their stories into pastiche poems, using "Jabberwocky" as their guide. A pastiche poem is a poem that honors the excellence of a poem by imitating its style or content. This style of poetry is a great starting place for students who may be new to poetry, because it provides them with a mentor text to rely upon. The selection of this text has the added bonus that the story it tells is a myth. Because students begin with stories from home, many of which will be myths or folktales, the selection of a myth in the format of a poem provides another layer of apprenticeship through the use of a mentor text.

Lesson Plan

This lesson is designed for a group of students enrolled in an on-level ninth grade English course in a suburban Texas, USA, high school. The languages represented in the classroom are English and Spanish, with approximately 20% nonnative English speakers. This high school offers English as a second or other language courses to replace English I and English II credits for students who are at beginning levels of English proficiency and have been in the country for 3 years or fewer. For this reason, the language proficiencies of ELs enrolled in the on-level English I course range from intermediate to advanced high. There is a mix of Hispanic, White, and African American students in the classroom. Many of the students in the course were from low socioeconomic backgrounds and were performing below level on standardized assessments. This class was a typical representation of the overall campus demographics.

This lesson is intended to support a diverse student group in analyzing poetry, identifying and using figurative language, and writing a poem in English. In the lesson, you will scaffold instruction to provide access to high-level language skills by utilizing cultural knowledge, community-based images, and mentor texts in poetry learning. In addition, you will entwine storytelling, photography, and poetry to help students meet the standards related to poetry analysis and writing. The final product in the lesson utilizes technology as a way to provide access for students to engage in poetry performance. The lesson focuses on meeting the targeted learning standards and incorporating language proficiency standards in the areas of listening, speaking, reading, writing, and viewing.

Lesson Plan Title	Teaching Poetry Through Attention to Language and Culture
Grade/Subject Area	Grade 9; English language arts
Duration	6 (45-minute) sessions
Proficiency Levels	Texas English Language Proficiency Standards: Intermediate to Advanced High (Texas Education Agency, 2011)

(continued on next page)

Lesson Plan *(continued)*	
Content Objectives	Students will analyze poetry, identify figurative language, and write a poem using a mentor text.
Content and Language Objectives	Students will be able to • analyze poetry, identify figurative language, and write a poem using a mentor text. (Content) • use a graphic organizer to organize the events in a poem while viewing a video illustrating the poem and collaborate with others to identify new vocabulary as the poem is analyzed in a whole group setting. (Language) • utilize a pastiche poetry framework to help them to create a poem using a familiar story and photographs labeled with descriptive language.
Alignment to Standards	**Texas Essential Knowledge & Skills** (Texas Education Code) • *§110.31(b)(3)*: Reading/Comprehension of Literary Text/Poetry. Students understand, make inferences and draw conclusions about the structure and elements of poetry and provide evidence from text to support their understanding. Students are expected to analyze the effects of diction and imagery (e.g., controlling images, figurative language, understatement, overstatement, irony, paradox) in poetry. • *§110.31(b)(14)(B)*: write a poem using a variety of poetic techniques (e.g., structural elements, figurative language) and a variety of poetic forms (e.g., sonnets, ballads). • *§110.36(c)(1)(C)*: give a presentation using informal, formal, and technical language effectively to meet the needs of audience, purpose, and occasion, employing eye contact, speaking rate such as pauses for effect, volume, enunciation, purposeful gestures, and conventions of language to communicate ideas effectively. **Texas English Language Proficiency Standards** (Texas Education Code) Intermediate Students • *§74.4(c)(4)(D)*: use prereading supports such as graphic organizers, illustrations, and pretaught topic-related vocabulary and other prereading activities to enhance comprehension of written text. • *§74.4(c)(4)(F)*: use visual and contextual support and support from peers and teachers to read grade-appropriate content area text, enhance and confirm understanding, and develop vocabulary, grasp of language structures, and background knowledge needed to comprehend increasingly challenging language. • *§74.4(c)(5)(B)*: write using newly acquired basic vocabulary and content-based grade-level vocabulary. Advanced/Advanced High Students • *§74.4(c)(4)(K)*: demonstrate English comprehension and expand reading skills by employing analytical skills such as evaluating written information and performing critical analyses commensurate with content area and grade-level needs. • *§74.4(c)(5)(G)*: narrate, describe, and explain with increasing specificity and detail to fulfill content area writing needs as more English is acquired.

(continued on next page)

Lesson Plan *(continued)*	
Outcomes	Students will • read a poem and analyze the text for structural elements, figurative language, and imagery with support from the teacher. • write a poem that incorporates structural elements, figurative language, and imagery.
Materials	• Anchor chart paper • "Jabberwocky" (Carroll, 2001) • Suggested texts for examples of storytelling (see Additional Resources) • Mobile device capable of taking photographs • Internet access • Projector and screen • Appendixes A–C (available on the companion website for this book): — Sequencing Graphic Organizer (Appendix A) — Sample final product (Appendix B) — Poetry Performance Rubric (Appendix C)

Highlighted Teaching Strategies

Though several strategies are used throughout the unit, the strategies that are the focus of instruction are

- valuing students' cultures,
- building background knowledge,
- providing comprehensible input,
- highlighting academic vocabulary, and
- scaffolding.

In the lesson, you focus on using stories that are familiar to students as a way to build background knowledge and value their out-of-school literacies. According to Johnson (1982), students are more effective at comprehending texts and mastering learning standards when the text is familiar or allows for interpretation by drawing on cultural context.

The lesson draws on one of Krashen's (2008) hypotheses when introducing the poem, "Jabberwocky." Krashen stated that when students are provided with comprehensible input, particularly in the form of reading, they perform at higher levels. In the lesson, you use varied multimedia paired with a graphic organizer to help students comprehend the nonsense language in the poem.

In English language teaching, researchers argue that explicit instruction is necessary to help students to master academic language, thereby leading to increased academic success (Tong, Lara-Alecio, Irby, Mathes, & Kwok, 2008). In this lesson, you segment the academic vocabulary into small chunks and teach the terms explicitly prior to proceeding with the lesson.

Additionally, you scaffold each portion of the learning so that students can rely on their out-of-school knowledge, dialogue, images, or graphic organizers to build that learning up to higher levels of complexity within the lesson. One of the scaffolding strategies used in this lesson is "turn and talk." In this strategy, students turn to someone sitting next to them to respond to a question you've posed or to discuss what they already know about a topic. This strategy allows students the opportunity to brainstorm with a peer prior to engaging in an activity.

Procedures

In preparation for this lesson, build background knowledge by explaining that many families have stories that they like to tell and that many of these stories are ghost stories, fables, myths, folktales, or family histories. At this point, introduce the key vocabulary: *storytelling* and *myth*.

To begin the discussion, provide an example by sharing a story from your own family. You can provide additional examples using picture books. (See the Additional Resources at the end of this chapter for a few suggestions.)

Next, draw a circle map on anchor chart paper. Ask the students to brainstorm—sharing stories that they are familiar with. Transcribe the students' ideas onto the circle map (see Figure 1 for an example of a completed circle map).

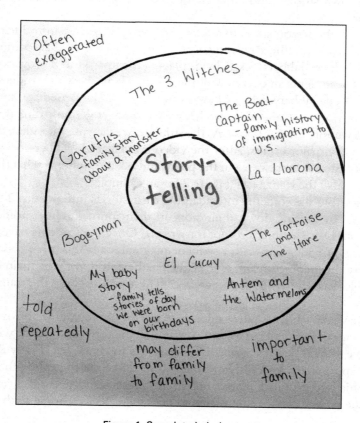

Figure 1. Completed circle map.

El Cucuy and the Boogeyman: A Multicultural Arts-Based Approach to Poetry

For homework that night, ask students to talk to their families about stories that are frequently told in their families. Each student should bring their favorite story example from their family to use in class. Stories in any language should be accepted.

When students return to class with their stories on Day 2, have them draw a picture to represent their story. The students should then label the picture with the words or images that they believe are most important to the story or that stand out to them as the most important. After the students have finished drawing, they partner up for the turn and talk; each partner will give a brief explanation of their story without telling the entire story.

The students then move from turn and talk to small collaborative groups you've assigned. Each student in the group should share their story with their small group. After each story, the students revisit their original drawing and add any new words or images that came up in their small group discussion. Once all group members have shared, they should select their favorite story from the group to be shared at closing, along with the drawing.

During the closing on Day 2, the selected students share their stories and drawings with the whole group and explain how they came up with the vocabulary they selected to label their drawing. As they listen, the rest of the class should write down any new vocabulary they hear modeled by their peers that they may want to use in their own stories. Add any new or interesting vocabulary to the circle map anchor chart.

On Day 3, the lesson shifts to a focus on poetry. Begin by introducing the academic vocabulary for the day: *event*, *stanza*, and *sequence*. Utilize comprehensible input to introduce "Jabberwocky," by displaying the image on the cover of the book and giving the students an overview of the poem. Then, show the students the YouTube video: "The Jabberwocky by Lewis Carroll – Read by Benedict Cumberbatch" (available at www.youtube.com/watch?v=Q_Um3787fSY; link directly from the companion website for this book). As the students are viewing the video, they should write down any major events. After the video is over, read "Jabberwocky" aloud to the students. Stop at each stanza in the poem and ask the students what they think is happening. Label the stanza (see Figure 2 for an example).

Next, scaffold the students into adapting their stories into poems. The students should begin by writing down their story in their journal. They should use their drawing from Day 2 as their prompt for writing. Once the students have completed their writing, provide them with a sequencing graphic organizer (Appendix A). The students use the graphic organizer to sequence their story into the main events, just as the whole class did with "Jabberwocky." These will become the stanzas of their own poem.

Next, have the students select a device to use for photography. I recommend that you encourage the students to use any device that they are comfortable with, but you should have several devices available for students to check out if they do not have their own appropriate device. The students use class time to explore the school for photographic opportunities that can be used to represent the major events in their story. At the end of class, ask students to take their devices home with them. The

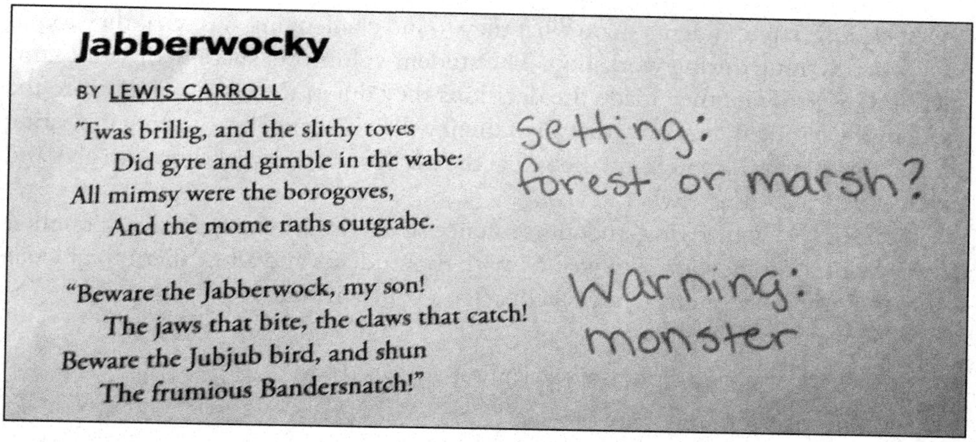

Jabberwocky

BY LEWIS CARROLL

'Twas brillig, and the slithy toves
    Did gyre and gimble in the wabe:
All mimsy were the borogoves,
    And the mome raths outgrabe.

"Beware the Jabberwock, my son!
    The jaws that bite, the claws that catch!
Beware the Jubjub bird, and shun
    The frumious Bandersnatch!"

Setting: forest or marsh?

Warning: monster

Figure 2. Annotating stanzas.

students complete their photograph collection by including images from their home or community. They should have a total of seven images, one for each stanza.

On Day 4, deepen the learning related to poetry. The academic language for the day is *figurative language, imagery, onomatopoeia, assonance,* and *portmanteau.* Guide students through analysis of the language in "Jabberwocky" one stanza at a time. Have the students identify which nonsense word in the poem is supposed to act as a noun, adjective, verb, and so on. Also encourage students to identify figurative language, such as onomatopoeia, assonance, and portmanteau. They may need more support at this point, because many of these concepts may be new to them. Color code the poem as students analyze the language, because this will provide students with a visual reference as they create the frameworks for their pastiche poems. Lead the students in discussing how the author used imagery and/or allusion for each stanza. Next, have students engage in another turn and talk, during which they will identify examples of imagery and/or allusion from the passage and what the author's purpose was in utilizing these techniques in his writing.

Next, select one stanza from "Jabberwocky." For example, you might select the first stanza that sets the scene. Use your own family story from Day 1 to model how to follow the author's style for creating a sense of setting in the first stanza. After you've completed modeling how to adapt a section of your story into a pastiche poem following "Jabberwocky," have students return to their seats to begin constructing their pastiche poems using the framework they created during the mini-lesson. First, they should align each stanza with an accompanying photograph from their collection. They should then break their story down into the appropriate stanzas. Once students have organized their poems into the general structure that they would like to use, they will begin to input their story into their framework.

While students are writing, conduct writing conferences with individual students and look for two to three good student examples for students to share during the day's closing. When you're selecting student work to share at closing, tell students what was valuable about their work sample and ask them if they feel comfortable sharing.

At closing, have students share what they found challenging and what they found easy when writing during workshop. The student volunteers share their work samples and discuss why they made the decisions they did in their writing. Prepare the students by letting them know that all of them will be sharing their writing in writing workshop the next day. Remind them that the purpose of the workshop is to give and receive feedback for use when revising.

Day 5 begins with giving students sentence stems for providing feedback on their peers' writing. Share your own writing with the students and allow them to practice using their sentence stems to give feedback on your writing.

Sentence Stem Examples:

- My favorite word/phrase/description you used was . . .

- This part reminded me of . . .

- This part/description/phrase made me feel . . .

- I was confused when . . .

- I wonder how you could . . .

- What would you think about . . .

- When comparing your writing to _____, I noticed _____ . . .

As the students practice using the sentence stems for providing feedback, give feedback to yourself on your own writing on the board, modeling how to take notes on the feedback so that you can use it for later editing and revision.

When moving students into writing workshop, it's helpful to arrange their seats into a circle, which facilitates discussion. Depending on the size of the class, you may choose to do one circle or you may break them into smaller circles, allowing enough time for each student to share and receive feedback. Students bring their sentence stems and their writing to the circle. Each student shares their current draft, and their peers will provide constructive feedback. Students should take notes when they receive feedback, as you modeled in the mini-lesson. Once each student has had an opportunity to share and receive feedback, all students go back to their seats to make any changes that they have decided to accept as they complete their final draft.

Closing

Day 6 focuses on putting the final draft of the pastiche poem and the photograph compilation into a final product using Haiku Deck (www.haikudeck.com). Haiku Deck is an online slideshow platform that focuses on the use of images. Introduce students to Haiku Deck and provide an example of what their final product might look like using your own story (Appendix B). Go through the basics of working in the application.

Once you've introduced the students to the functionality of Haiku Deck, have them input their photographs into the platform. Haiku Deck limits the amount of text per slide, so students should go back to their brainstorming notes in which they selected descriptive language to represent the major events of the story. They should compare these terms to the language they used in their stanzas and determine which words they want to use to emphasize their artwork. They will add these words to their slides.

Once students have completed their presentation in Haiku Deck, they return to their small groups from the initial lesson to practice performing. Their peers give them feedback on their performance, until each student is reasonably comfortable with putting their performance together.

Extensions

For students who are working at more advanced levels of English proficiency, this lesson can easily be extended to deepen the exploration of figurative language and poetic form. Students could also be given the opportunity to go beyond poetry performance to have the opportunity to publish their work in a classroom anthology or an online platform. You could also encourage students to move past the pastiche poem to creating something original using images that they find in their community.

Caveats

This lesson is most appropriate for students at intermediate to advanced high levels of English language proficiency. The linguistic challenge presented in the poetry analysis would need further accommodation to be appropriate for students at beginning levels of English.

Assessment and Evaluation

On Day 7, students engage in a poetry performance to showcase the work that they completed in this unit. This performance helps to validate student writing and provides an authentic audience. Additionally, an assessment that uses poetry performance reflects the oral tradition of storytelling that students explored at the beginning of the unit. This approach provides students with an opportunity to practice speaking standards in addition to the reading and writing standards that were the focus of the lesson. The two recommended audience variations are as follows:

- Audience Option 1: The students' families are invited to come in during class, so that students can honor their families by turning their family stories into art.

- Audience Option 2: A venue within the community is selected, such as a popular restaurant, coffeehouse, or park. Students host an "Open Mic" night in which they perform their own poems along with their digital presentations, but also invite others from the community to share their own writing. NOTE: For this option, you will need to verify that the location has the appropriate equipment for students to share their Haiku Deck as the students are performing their poems. This also requires parent permission.

For assessment of the content standards, use a rzubric to evaluate the students' mastery (Appendix C).

Reflection on and Analysis of the Lesson

In Walker's (2017) study of the English language teaching practices of high-quality middle schools, she found that some schools hosted community literacy or writing nights, rather than traditional dinners or culture nights. These events were held in common spaces within the community, such as coffee shops, and highlighted the stories and writing produced within the community. The schools that employed community literacy events reported that EL engagement increased with in-school literacy activities as a result of providing a space to value students' out-of-school literacies. The culmination of this lesson goes beyond leveraging home language and literacies in the classroom to celebrating the combined in- and out-of-school language and literacies of all students.

Because this lesson utilizes stories that are important to students and shares their personal writing, it is key to the success of the lesson that a safe classroom environment has been well-established. According to Bondy, Ross, Gallingane, and Hambacher (2007), attention should be paid to developing caring relationships, established expectations, student accountability, and culturally responsive communication when working to create positive classroom environments.

This lesson is an excellent approach for engaging high school ELs in poetry writing and analysis because employing storytelling as the foundation for the lesson is the first step in creating a third space in the classroom. Beginning with stories from students' homes demonstrates the value of out-of-school literacies from the start. Additionally, the use of photography linguistically accommodates the instruction by providing students with visual representations of text and visual scaffolds for their own writing.

English language educators are encouraged to find creative ways to incorporate arts-based instruction as one approach for supporting the literacy and language development of high school ELs. By rethinking ways of knowing and understanding language and literacy instruction, English language educators can increase their pedagogic repertoires, thereby expanding their ability to meet the specific needs of the high school ELs with whom they have been entrusted.

The appendixes and additional resources for this chapter are available at www.tesol.org/practices-highschool.

Katie Walker is an assistant professor of literacy and ESOL at Coastal Carolina University, South Carolina, USA.

References

Bondy, E., Ross, D. D., Gallingane, C., & Hambacher, E. (2007). Creating environments of success and resilience: Culturally responsive classroom management and more. *Urban Education, 42*(4), 326–348.

Cahnmann-Taylor, M., Bleyle, S., Hwang, Y., & Zhang, K. (2017). Teaching poetry in TESOL teacher education: Heightened attention to language as well as to cultural and political critique through poetry writing. *TESOL Journal, 8*, 70–101. doi:10.1002/tesj.263

Carroll, L. (2001). *Jabberwocky and other poems*. Mineola, NY: Dover.

Chappell, S., & Faltis, C. (2013). *The arts and emergent bilingual youth: Building critical, creative programs in school and community contexts*. New York, NY: Routledge.

Dabach, D. (2010). Visual prompts in writing instruction: Working with middle school English language learners. In J. Donahue & J. Stuart (Eds.), *Artful teaching: Integrating the arts for understanding across the curriculum, K–8* (pp. 103–110). New York, NY: Teachers College Press.

Friesen, H. L. (2012). Photography and writing: Alternative ways of learning for ESL students. *Teaching English in the two-year college, 40*(1), 39–43.

García, O. (2009). Emergent bilinguals and TESOL: What's in a name? *TESOL Quarterly, 43*, 322–326.

Johnson, P. (1982). Effects on reading comprehension of building background knowledge. *TESOL Quarterly, 16*, 503–516.

Krashen, S. (2008). Language education: Past, present, and future. *Language Education, 39*(2), 178–187.

Moje, E. B., Ciechanowski, K. M., Kramer, K., Ellis, L., Carrillo, R., & Collazo, T. (2004). Working toward the third space in content area literacy: An examination of everyday funds of knowledge and discourse. *Reading Research Quarterly, 39*(1), 38–70.

Moore, J. N. (2002). Practicing poetry: Teaching to learn and learning to teach. *English Journal, 91*(3), 44–50. doi:10.2307/821511

Perry, K. H. (2008). From storytelling to writing: Transforming literacy practices among Sudanese refugees. *Journal of Literacy Research, 40*, 317–358.

Pratt, M. L. (1991). Arts of the contact zone. In P. Franklin (Ed.), *Profession '91* (pp. 33–40). New York, NY: Modern Language Association.

Texas Education Agency. (2011). TELPAS Resources. Austin, TX: Author. Retrieved from https://tea.texas.gov/student.assessment/ell/telpas/

Texas Education Code §110. Texas Essential Knowledge and Skills for English Language Arts and Reading. Chapter 74, Subchapter C. High School.

Texas Education Code §74.4.d. English Language Proficiency Standards. Chapter 74, Subchapter A. Required Curriculum.

Tong, F., Lara-Alecio, R., Irby, B., Mathes, P., & Kwok, O. (2008). Accelerating early academic oral English development in transitional bilingual and structure English immersion programs. *American Educational Research Journal, 45*(4), 1011–1044.

Walker, M. K. (2017). *Texas schools to watch and middle-level ESL programs: A multiple case study* (Doctoral dissertation). Retrieved from ProQuest Dissertations & Theses Global. (UMI No. 1937577399)

Additional Resources

Hayes, J. (2001). *El cucuy: A bogeyman cuento*. El Paso, TX: Cinco Puntos Press.

Hayes, J. (2006). *La llorona: The weeping woman*. El Paso, TX: Cinco Puntos Press.

Morien Jones (Producer). (2015, July 7). Jabberwocky by Lewis Carroll—read by Benedict Cumberbatch [Video File]. Retrieved from https://www.youtube.com/watch?v=Q_Um3787fSY

Parks, B. (1998). *Psssst! It's me the bogeyman*. New York, NY: Atheneum.

Thomas, J. C. (2006). *The three witches*. New York, NY: Harper Collins.

3

Translanguaging to Support Reading and Writing Engagement in the English Language Arts Classroom

Seth M. Ross, Mary Amanda Stewart

Introduction

The notion of translanguaging is fairly new in U.S. educational contexts, and there is currently little research to illustrate how translanguaging might take place in an English-medium secondary classroom (cf. Ebe & Chapman-Santiago, 2016; García, Flores, Chu, 2011; García, Johnson, & Seltzer, 2017; Seltzer, Collins, & Angeles, 2016). In this chapter, we use García and Li Wei's (2014) definition of translanguaging to describe how bilinguals draw from all of their languages to make meaning, and we focus on emergent bilingual high school seniors in an English language arts (ELA) classroom. We choose to not describe this classroom as English-only, because the teacher has purposefully adopted a translanguaging stance, but rather call it an English-medium classroom (García et al., 2017), where the official curriculum and assessment measures for this course are in English. We ground our classroom research in the belief that all languages are valuable and needed for effective learning and that preventing students from drawing from their full linguistic repertoires is like putting them in an English straightjacket (Cook, 2001), especially when they need to engage in complex texts and ideas primarily presented in the second language (L2).

Consequently, the TESOL article inspiring the lesson shared in this chapter presents innovative research from the elementary English-medium classroom to investigate how teachers provide regular effective scaffolding to make translanguaging a normative classroom practice. Drawing from the ideas in this article, this chapter's lesson illustrates how the same principles can be enacted in the last year of secondary schooling, 12th grade, in an ELA classroom for students who are receiving language support services in their school. If these research-based practices can be applied from early elementary school (original research) to the 12th grade, then surely all high school teachers can put them into practice in their own classrooms to support learners at all levels of English language acquisition.

The lesson highlighted in this chapter is the product of the teacher's (first author Seth) purposeful and systematic response from learning about the theory and research support for translanguaging through graduate coursework with the second author (Mary Amanda). Seth is an experienced English as a second language, reading, and ELA teacher who has worked with high school students considered emergent bilinguals for over a decade. Although his first and primary language is English, he is from a city on the U.S./Mexican border where he grew up surrounded by the Spanish language and understood the importance of being bilingual. Through coursework as a young adult, he formally acquired Spanish as an L2 and is fairly fluent in conversational and academic language. Therefore, like the students in his class who began acquiring their L2, English, as young adults, Seth can be described as a sequential bilingual (Baker & Wright, 2017). The students in the classroom are all English/Spanish bilinguals who moved to the United States 4–5 years before entering this senior English class. They were with the same teacher for ninth and 11th grade English, and have thus built strong relationships with him. All of the students are from the Latin American countries of Mexico, Cuba, Honduras, and El Salvador. Their English proficiency levels range from intermediate to advanced, and their Spanish proficiency levels are all advanced in oral language and intermediate to advanced in reading and writing as a result of the school's excellent Spanish for Spanish speakers courses that the students have taken. Many of them also came to the United States with high levels of Spanish literacy because of their education in the home country.

Seth naturally knew that his students' first languages (L1s) were resources he could leverage for L2 learning and for years would encourage their presence in his English classroom. Indeed, his experience is similar to that referenced by other researchers as they introduce the idea of translanguaging to some teachers: "When we first introduce translanguaging, educators who have a child-centered educational philosophy get it. Many say they have been doing it for years but have not had a name for it nor had been given permission to do so" (García & Kleyn, 2016a, p. 15). Thus, he had a version of a translanguaging classroom for years before he learned about the term in the Fall 2017 semester as he took his first graduate course in his Masters of Reading Education program. Through this course, he began to understand why what he naturally felt led to do was beneficial to his emergent bilingual students and began thinking more systematically about why, how, and when he could encourage and model language other than English use in his ELA classroom.

Besides the immediate academic benefits, translanguaging also allows students to learn how to leverage their languages beyond the high school walls. U.S. 12th-grade students need to be prepared to make their own way in a U.S. college or university where most (if not all) of the coursework will be in English. They also need the skills to successfully enter the U.S. workforce and be productive citizens in their new country, all requiring the ability to navigate multiple challenges. Thus, creating a translanguaging classroom has various benefits for Seth's students. While simultaneously receiving English IV credit, increasing their L2 proficiency, and developing their overall literacy skills, students are also learning how they can leverage their knowledge of their L1, learning acquired in their L1, and understandings about language and literacy for their success.

The lesson in this chapter took place in the Spring 2018 semester, after the teacher, Seth, had completed one semester of coursework focusing on L2 acquisition and bilingual theories, with a focus on creating a translanguaging classroom (García et al., 2017). In Seth's class, he guides students to draw from all of their languages to engage with complex text in English, specifically the prologue to the novel *The Distance Between Us*, by Reyna Grande (2012), which they used as a mentor text (Culham, 2014). The goal of this was for the students to write their own memoirs.

Synopsis of Original Research

Daniel, S. M., Jiménez, R. T., Pray, L., & Pacheco, M. B. (2017). Scaffolding to make translanguaging a classroom norm. *TESOL Journal*. Advance online publication. doi:10.1002/tesj.361

The term *translanguaging* was first coined by Williams (1996) in his study of bilingual (Welsh/English) children's use of language in school. More recently, García and colleagues (e.g., García et al., 2017; García & Kleyn, 2016b; García & Menken, 2015) have brought the term to classroom settings in the United States, disrupting a language separation mentality that has long dominated classroom learning. (See Additional Resources for more information on their work, or link directly from the companion website for this book). Much research regarding translanguaging has focused on the elementary dual language or bilingual classroom where there are two official languages present (e.g., García-Mateus & Palmer, 2017; Gort, 2006; Hopewell, 2017); however, there is also promising research that describes examples of translanguaging in the general high school classroom (García et al., 2011; Stewart & Hansen-Thomas, 2016). In the anchor article, Daniel et al. (2017) explain how translanguaging can be approached through a constructivist stance as a way of being, doing, and learning in the classroom, rather than a single strategy employed at specific times. They study how monolingual second- and third-grade teachers model how to engage in translanguaging practices to increase literacy and language learning for their Spanish- and Arabic-speaking students. The authors are particularly interested in how translanguaging might look in what they call English-only classrooms—how teachers, students, and all other stakeholders might view translanguaging as regular literacy instruction. The article provides scaffolding examples of these teachers' purposeful use of translanguaging in their ELA classrooms.

Much like Seth, the elementary teachers in the article first learned about the concept of translanguaging, understanding what it is, why it could be beneficial, and how it connects to constructivist literacy pedagogy before purposefully applying it to their classrooms. Through design-based research, the researchers studied their teacher participants and their classrooms to determine how educators can further the discussion of how to effectively create a translanguaging classroom, particularly in English-medium settings. Their initial findings from this ongoing work are presented in the *TESOL Journal* article as three general recommendations.

First, teachers might need to integrate students' use of languages other than English as a resource in the classroom by directly asking them to use the languages. Because the young students in the study had been conditioned to view school as an English-only context, the teachers first had to ask the students to use their L1s, Spanish and Arabic, in the literacy classroom where English was the primary means of instruction and assessment. Even though the teachers did not speak the students' L1s, they encouraged them to translate or "write across their languages" (p. 6) when learning. They modeled how this can be a powerful tool for learning and overtly tried to show the children that their languages were valued in their classrooms.

Next, Daniel et al. (2017) suggested that teachers can set conditions for students to naturally bring in their home literacy practices. The teachers in the research purposefully leveraged their students' experiences of living bilingually and regularly serving as translators or language brokers (Tse, 1996) with friends at school, in their communities, or at home. Many children and youth in the dynamic process of acquiring English as a second or additional language regularly perform these advanced tasks in their lives (Orellana, 2009), yet rarely receive recognition for it or instruction on how to capitalize on these skills in the school (Dorner, Orellana, & Jiménez, 2008). The teachers prompted students to discuss when, how, and for whom they have translated and encouraged them to do the same in the classroom for greater literacy learning.

Finally, the researchers (Daniel et al., 2017) recommend that teachers approach translanguaging as routine scaffolding as they focus on the learning process over correctness. To illustrate, understanding that these elementary children had probably not received formal literacy instruction in their L1, the teachers encouraged the students to write words from their L1 even if they did not know the correct letter/sound correspondence. For example, after hearing students say "I speak Spanish" and "I speak Arabic" in their own languages, the teachers used the English alphabet to write those phrases, asking the students to do the same. This concept is called transliteration—writing a word in one language by using the letter/sound correspondence from another alphabet—and is often used when using two languages with different scripts. The teachers in the study modeled this for their students, showing them that learning is a problem-solving experience.

The researchers (Daniel et al., 2017) referred to these strategies as designed-in scaffolding that seeks to make drawing from all of one's languages a regular part of classroom literacy learning, rather than a particular strategy to be implemented. It is crucial to note that for the teachers to do this effectively, they needed to understand the theory, research, and tenets of translanguaging. This allowed them to combine that new learning with their own pedagogical and content knowledge as well as their awareness of their own students. This resulted in the teachers possessing the necessary knowledge to determine how to create a translanguaging classroom through "thoughtful scaffolding" to best meet the needs of their unique students.

Rationale

As the authors emphasize in the original research, there is certainly a dearth of scholarly work to give teachers ideas of what translanguaging might look like in the English-only or, as we prefer to call it, English-medium classroom. Surely, the emergent bilingual 12th-grade students in these lessons and in high schools in general have a wealth of knowledge of their L1 and experiences that might be best communicated in that language. Furthermore, they need to have opportunities to learn how they can leverage all of their languages for their gain both in and out of the classroom.

It is important to note that translanguaging is more than allowing students to use their L1 or tolerating the presence of languages other than English. For example, Stewart and Hansen-Thomas (2016) encourage teachers to sanction a space for translanguaging in the high school ELA classroom as they use poetry composition to accomplish that goal. Daniel et al. (2017) suggest teachers make translanguaging a classroom norm through ongoing scaffolding techniques. This works toward viewing literacy instruction, even at the level of Senior English, through a multilingual lens, replacing longstanding norms of monolingual views that ultimately harm multilingual students (Hopewell, 2017).

Au (1998) explains that constructivist literacy teachers of culturally and linguistically diverse learners should emphasize the students themselves taking ownership of their learning. This chapter's lesson exemplifies this concept in how the teacher sets the conditions for the young adult students to decide when and how to use Spanish to further their understanding of complex text in English, their L2. This is important because these students will hopefully graduate high school the same semester and explore options in the workforce and/or in postsecondary education. They need the skills to make sense of written and oral language as well as other forms of communication by using all of their linguistic resources.

Also following a constructivist paradigm, it is crucial that teachers are empowered to make well-planned as well as on-the-spot curricular and instructional decisions within their classrooms that are meaningful and effective for their particular situations. Unlike in a behaviorist model that might give teachers a list of specific strategies to use, this lesson plan follows the idea of the original research—that researchers and teacher educators must recognize and value the knowledge that classroom teachers possess, particularly the insights they have from being in the classroom and developing relationships with the students and families they serve. This chapter is evidence of how the teacher first learned about translanguaging and then made his own purposeful decisions in how to employ these ideas in his classroom based on his knowledge of the content area; effective pedagogical practices; and, most important, his students' lives, strengths, needs, and resources. Finally, the teacher took that combination of knowledge and applied an understanding of translanguaging to consider how to model those strategies with his students. Through the lesson in this chapter, we hope to impact other school/university partnerships to engage in learning from one another as researchers show a high regard for the work teachers are regularly doing in their classrooms.

Lesson Plan

Lesson Plan Title	The Power of One Person's Story
Grade/Subject	Grade 12; English language arts
Duration	2 (90-minute) class periods
Proficiency Levels	• Texas English Language Proficiency Standards (Texas Education Agency, 2011): Intermediate to Advanced • WIDA (2012): Levels 3–5 (Developing to Bridging)
Content and Language Objectives	Students will be able to • determine the theme of the text and support their conclusion with evidence. (Content) • analyze the structure of the text and how the author used language to communicate his or her ideas. (Content) • follow the style and genre of a memoir to write a prologue to their own memoir. (Content) • write the prologue to their own memoir using new vocabulary in English to explain their experiences. (Language) • reflect upon their writing with peers and the teacher to improve their work in preparation for publication. (Language)
Alignment to Standards	**Texas Essential Knowledge and Skills** (Texas Education Code, §110.34) • *(b)(6)*: Reading/Comprehension of Literary Text/Literary Nonfiction. Students understand, make inferences and draw conclusions about the varied structural patterns and features of literary nonfiction and provide evidence from text to support their understanding. Students are expected to analyze the effect of ambiguity, contradiction, subtlety, paradox, irony, sarcasm, and overstatement in literary essays, speeches, and other forms of literary nonfiction. • *(b)(13)*: Writing/Writing Process. Students use elements of the writing process (planning, drafting, revising, editing, and publishing) to compose text. Students are expected to: — *(A)*: plan a first draft by selecting the correct genre for conveying the intended meaning to multiple audiences, determining appropriate topics through a range of strategies (e.g., discussion, background reading, personal interests, interviews), and developing a thesis or controlling idea. • *(b)(14)*: Writing/Literary Texts. Students write literary texts to express their ideas and feelings about real or imagined people, events, and ideas. Students are responsible for at least two forms of literary writing. Students are expected to: — *(A)*: write an engaging story with a well-developed conflict and resolution, a clear theme, complex and non-stereotypical characters, a range of literary strategies (e.g., dialogue, suspense), devices to enhance the plot, and sensory details that define the mood or tone.

(continued on next page)

Lesson Plan *(continued)*	
Alignment to Standards *(continued)*	**Common Core State Standards** (National Governors Association Center for Best Practices & Council of Chief State School Officers, 2017) • *CCSS.ELA-LITERACY.RL.11-12.1*: Cite strong and thorough textual evidence to support analysis of what the text says explicitly as well as inferences drawn from the text, including determining where the text leaves matters uncertain. • *CCSS.ELA-LITERACY.W.11-12.3*: Write narratives to develop real or imagined experiences or events using effective technique, well-chosen details, and well-structured event sequences.
Outcomes	Student will • discuss and analyze a text with evidence to support their conclusions. • write prologues to their own memoir. • publish their prologues on a shared class website.
Materials	• Highlighters • Post-it notes • Class set of *The Distance Between Us: Young Adult Edition* (Grande, 2017) • Copy of the prologue from *The Distance Between Us* (Grande, 2012; this is the original version for annotation and analysis with highly complex text) • Computers for word processing and internet access • Writing notebooks

Highlighted Teaching Strategies

Culturally relevant literature, shared reading, the use of translanguaging, whole-class and small group interaction, and writer's workshop are all strategies used during the lesson. In this chapter, culturally relevant literature means using texts to which the reader might have a strong personal connection. The teacher decided to use the memoir The Distance Between Us: Young Adult Edition (Grande, 2017) because the majority of the students in the class had shared experiences of separation from their parents, immigration to a new country, and strong emotions about their family's decision to move to the United States. He determined that Grande's (2012; 2017) writing would speak to his students on a personal level, motivate them to engage in and value literacy, and serve as a springboard for them to mimic the memoir genre.

Using shared reading to provide students both the visual and aural cues, the teacher read aloud the prologue of the original *The Distance Between Us* (Grande, 2012) while students followed along, highlighting lines that stood out to them. Students highlighted lines they determined were important to the message of the text or demonstrated powerful and desirable writing that effectively communicated the author's message. Prior to this lesson, the class had practiced how to read both like readers and writers, to analyze textual meaning, and to mimic craft moves in their own writing. Students were prompted to respond to the following questions

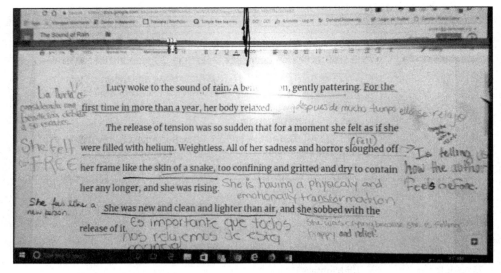

Figure 1. Whole-class analysis of text in English and Spanish.

throughout the shared reading of the prologue: "What do you notice?," "What lines spoke powerfully to you?," and "Why do you think the writer made that choice?" Translanguaging was evident throughout the lessons as students utilized their L1, Spanish, to discuss and analyze the text in depth with one another in small groups as well as a whole class (see Figure 1). Thus, they used both English and Spanish to facilitate comprehension of the text, analyze for deeper meaning, and discuss the text in depth.

Students also engaged translanguaging to plan, structure, develop, and produce a prologue to their own memoir, using both languages to facilitate their writing, although the final product was primarily in English. As a whole class, the teacher and students discussed the writing moves used by Grande (2012) and how they might mimic or use them in their own writing. The teacher wrote his own prologue to mentor them through the writer's process.

Using tenets of the writer's workshop (Leer & Runck, 2016), the teacher also conferenced with students individually throughout the drafting process, during which time both students and teacher utilized English and Spanish to talk about their writing, provide one another feedback, ask questions, make decisions, and improve their craft. While some students were in a writer's conference with the teacher, others used Chromebooks to type their second draft in anticipation of further conferencing and eventual publication of their writing.

Procedures

First class session

Begin by passing out copies of the prologue to *The Distance Between Us* (2012) and asking students what they know about the memoir genre. In Seth's class, students responded with "It sounds like memory," "It is something they remember?," and, "Is it about a person's history or *cuento* [story]?" Have students listen as you read, following along in their own copy, highlighting lines that speak to them or stand out. They should have practiced these skills in prior class sessions, and so be able to take note of what they determine to be significant and write about their noticings on their copy of the text. Throughout this process, students speak with each other in English and Spanish about the prologue, making sense of the text, and talking about what the author is trying to communicate.

Next, ask students about what they noticed and have them come up to the board and underline text, explaining why they think the lines are significant or meaningful. In Seth's class, some of the students wrote the following statements that the class discussed:

- "One grandmother just mention unrealistic thing like '*La Llorona*'[1] ['The Weeping Woman']. *Abuela* [Grandmother] Chinta talks more realistic."
- "*Abuela* [Grandmother] Evila tries to scare them with unrealistic things."
- "*El Otro Lado* [The Other Side] is like death, you never see them again."

This final comment explained the symbolism of the United States to the author and other residents of Guerrero, Mexico, the state in Mexico where the book begins. Two of the students were from Guerrero, and spoke about how many people had left their region of Mexico to come to the United States, and that many *abuelas* [grandmothers] and *tías* [aunts] cared for children, receiving money from their parents in the United States. A student who had not yet replied added her clarification, "So a memoir is a memory about someone's life?" She was supported by another student who told her "It's a memory or *memoria* of her life." She then asked, "Is this a true story or fiction?"

Without directly answering the questions, give the students their own copy of the young adult version of the book in English and allow the students to discover by looking at the cover and reading the back that the book is a true account of the author's life. End the class by coming to a shared understanding that memoir is the account of the author, according to his or her perspective, and is based upon one's life experiences.

Second class session

Have students take out their annotated copies of the prologue to *The Distance Between Us* (2012) and begin to examine the text as writers. Students discuss, in both English and Spanish, how the author purposefully contrasted the two grandmothers to get the reader to focus on how she thinks of both of them. In Seth's class, the following dialogue occurred:

Isis[2]: She wants us to know that *Abuela* [Grandmother] Evila tries to scare them, *Abuela* [Grandmother] Chinta tries to inspire them, but she is realistic. She knows they are just stories. Her truth is separation.

Mayra: But the grandmothers are important to her or she wouldn't say anything about them.

---

[1] La Llorona is a common story that adults tell children in Mexico and many other parts of Latin America.
[2] All student names are pseudonyms.

Isis:	But she knows that *El Otro Lado* [The Other Side] is more powerful than *las abuelas* [the grandmothers]. It took her dad and now it is going to take her mom.
Tania:	She makes *El Otro Lado* [The Other Side] seem scary and powerful like *La Llorona y La Virgen* (The Weeping Woman and The Virgin).

After students finish their conversations (in English and/or Spanish) in small groups about the writing, projected your own prologue to your memoir to serve as another mentor text to students as they write their own. Place it side-by-side with Grande's (2012) to show students how you have mimicked her style, but made it your own. Students may ask if they have to follow her structure and style exactly; let them know they should make their prologue their own, utilizing the writer's choices they see as most appropriate, but should have a focus on staying within the genre of memoir in their own prologue. Seth chose to do this because he believes it is vital that teachers write alongside their students, to experience what they go through, understanding the process students will be asked to engage in. Writing your own prologue will help him design the writing assignment and ensure that you under-stands the writer's experience. It also allows students to see that you value writing, and that you do not just assign tasks, but believe passionately in the power of writing and its part in everyone's lives.

Students should then begin to write their own memoirs as you meet with each of them, checking on their progress, answering questions, and helping them focus their ideas to begin the writing process. Some students may already have ideas from prior writings in their writer's notebook, if you use one regularly in class. Seth's student Tania powerfully wrote about a life-changing diagnosis and how the adverse situation has changed the course of her life. As evident in the following unedited text of her rough draft, she felt liberated to use both Spanish and English as guided by the mentor text. This illustrates translanguaging in her writing as she draws from all of her languages.

> One day changed my life, I did not know if it was for good or for bad, but that day I thought I was going to die. That day was August 4, 2017,when I was diagnosed with a disease in the brain that there is no cure, only medicine to control it.

> When I thought that everything was over to me, my world collapsed, my mom was the person who gave me support to keep going and a sentence that she told me, that today is in my mind, "Despues de la tormenta, sale el sol—After the storm the sun comes up."

> A few months ago my dream was to study to be a chef, but after my life changed and now I have the clarity that I want to be a neurologist and help all the people, help as they need and not like me just for not having insurance and a social security number, not one wanted to help me, but I found a doctor who did not care about that and helped me.

> Now I know what I want in my life and I know that what I have is
> not an impediment to keep going. I do not know why this happened
> to me, but what I do not know is where i am going and where I want
> to go and that "Los tiempos de Dios son muy buenos—God's times
> are very good."

Other students may struggle to begin and need to conference with you to organize their ideas and begin the process. Others may keep their writing process hidden from you until they are ready to reveal it, only allowing you to see that they are indeed making progress, but not requiring a conference until they have completed a draft. Throughout this process, students should speak, write, listen, and read using both their L1 and L2. Seth's students used Spanish, their L1, to clarify the meaning of the English text, discuss with one another or the teacher how to best describe their intended meaning in English, or to consult a translator or dictionary. Such regular and purposeful use of students' L1 provides them essential scaffolding to engage successfully in the learning.

As class ends, students turn in their drafts or take them home to complete by the next class meeting. Students may make appointments to see you for guidance with their writing. Because writing is a dynamic process, students at multiple levels of English proficiency will need various supports as they demonstrate different abilities within different genres. Your emergent bilinguals should have a final deadline to submit their drafts, but they should not feel pressured to perform within timed parameters, allowing them to focus on the process individually instead of on an arbitrary timeline that applies to all learners. Thus, the second class should end with some students turning in their drafts, others taking them home to finish, and still other students making appointments to have another writing conference.

Extensions

The reading portion of the lesson (Day 1) can extend by having students bring in related texts that connect to what they have read, or memoirs from other sources. (See Additional Resources for specific suggestions of memoirs.) Students can share these selections with each other, expanding their own literary world to include a more diverse collection of voices. Additionally, the most logical extension is for the students to continue reading the young reader's edition of the novel, which Seth's students do for the remainder of the instructional unit, using a combination of shared reading (Seth reads out loud while students follow along) and independent reading. Each chapter can be full of informal discussion and journal writing, which can occur in all of students' languages to help them make the most meaning from the text. Some students might also want to read parts or all of the book in their L1, Spanish, or in more complex English; the book comes in three versions: The young readers edition in English and the original version in both English and Spanish.

Extension ideas for the writing portion of the lesson (Day 2) include a full student memoir, building on the prologue. Students can complete their stories and share their narratives with others. Publication of their memoirs would also be a welcome extension that would foster a higher quality of writing, empower students by sharing their stories, and value their work beyond the school setting. Publication could occur on a class website, in a class book, or be narrated aloud as a podcast or a StoryCorps style production (https://storycorps.org). In a newcomer English class, this would be a great opportunity for students to share their recent immigration stories, including illustrations, pictures, images, or original artwork to help readers understand their journals even more deeply.

Caveats

Though this lesson was carried out with emergent bilinguals who spoke English and Spanish, it could also apply to classrooms with multiple L1s. In another one of Seth's ELA classes, students who speak Tagalog, Wolof, Spanish, Vietnamese, and Urdu have been able to leverage their L1 to speak with other students as they discuss text and participate in writer's workshop, helping each other to comprehend, analyze, plan, and write using their L1. Although Seth speaks Spanish, which certainly aided in his use of translanguaging, there is evidence from research that teachers can create a translanguaging classroom regardless of the languages they do or do not speak (e.g., see Chapters 5 and 7 of this book for further examples).

Another caveat to consider is the personal nature of the memoir genre. When choosing the text for this lesson, be cognizant of your students, their experiences, and any possible responses that might arise as a result of the topics in the text. Knowing your students and having a strong relationship with them will aid you in selecting texts and topics that will not elicit negative responses or cause students to relive traumas. Finally, even though Seth's lesson took place in a classroom with students with higher levels of English language proficiency, the lesson could also be used with beginning-level students, with a different text and more scaffolds to help them produce writing and express themselves both linguistically and artistically.

Assessment and Evaluation

Preassessment can consist of prior lessons using reader's workshop (Kittle, 2013) or writer's workshop to gauge students' linguistic proficiency levels and determine the text and its difficulty level and whether students would be able to proficiently write in the selected genre. Figure 2 demonstrates a prior reader's workshop lesson in which students utilized translanguaging to analyze what a previous text was communicating. This allowed the teacher to determine students' abilities to analyze the focal text in Lesson 1 in small groups.

During the reading portion of the lesson (Class 1), you can assess student performance by paying close attention to whole-class and small group discussion, reading student annotation and reflection on their copies of the prologue, and observing their overall interaction with the text. Students should engage in all of these using both English and Spanish to leverage their understanding and analysis.

During the writing portion of the lesson (Class 2), you can assess students by conferencing with them throughout the process. You can measure their linguistic proficiency; provide immediate feedback; and apply individual, small group, or whole-class scaffolds during this class period. Individual scaffolds may include a quick mini-lesson about imagery, past tense verb tense, or use of the L1 to jumpstart a reluctant writer. For example, when Seth's student Sara was struggling to get started,

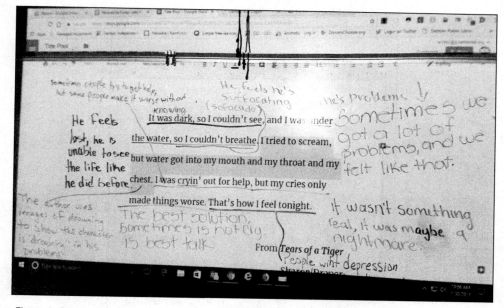

Figure 2. Group work from students using all of their languages to analyze a text prior to the lesson.

having her sit at the conference table and write in Spanish helped her to overcome her English language writer's block (see Figure 3). She and Seth determined that she would publish her memoir in both Spanish and English. Ongoing, informal, and formative assessment allows teachers to make student-centered instructional choices such as this one.

Small-group scaffolds can be used when you observe a pattern in student writing. For example, with shifting verb tenses you could respond by pulling selected students aside, giving examples, and providing a low-risk way to revise and edit throughout the writing process. When Seth's student Yohana shared her writing with him, she was using both present tense and past tense in the same sentence. They read the sentence out loud together and Seth asked her what she thought might need to change—what sounded weird. After hearing the sentence, she was immediately able to correct the verb tense error. Often, when students read their writing out loud, they hear the mistakes that they did not when reading silently.

Whole-class scaffolds can be used when you notice the entire class struggling with a concept: You can give a mini-lesson to address what you observe, providing students with a quick way to fill in the gaps and successfully engage with the lesson. During Seth's lesson, these were minor, focusing on using commas in a series and avoiding run-on sentences.

Postassessment consists of providing individual writing conferences with each student. In these conferences, they read their writing with you, make decisions about how they can edit it, and receive guidance prior to grading. You should continuously strive to emphasize to your students that writing is a process, and they will complete many iterations of a writing assignment for publication before they submit it. Following is an example of what Seth refers to as an initial, revised draft in his writer's

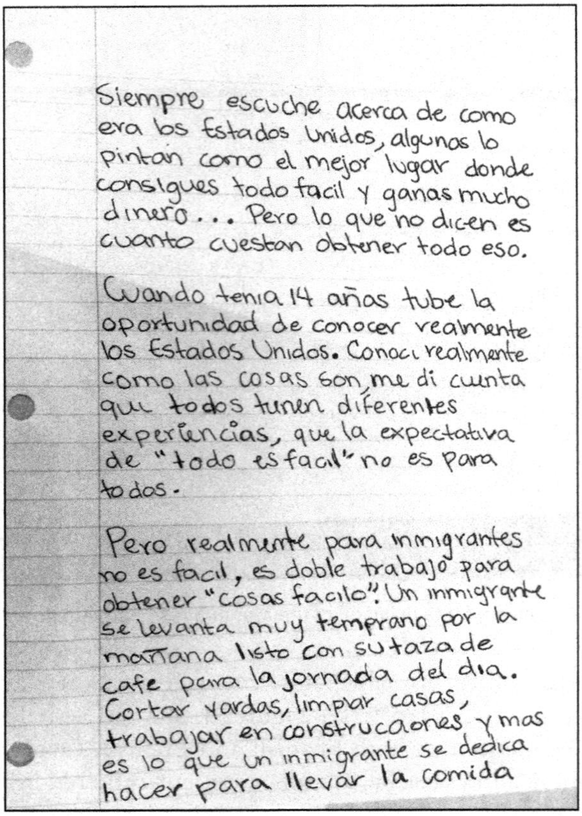
Siempre escuche acerca de como
era los Estados Unidos, algunos lo
pintan como el mejor lugar donde
consigues todo facil y ganas mucho
dinero... Pero lo que no dicen es
cuanto cuestan obtener todo eso.

Cuando tenia 14 años tube la
oportunidad de conocer realmente
los Estados Unidos. Conoci realmente
como las cosas son, me di cuenta
que todos tienen diferentes
experiencias, que la expectativa
de "todo es facil" no es para
todos.

Pero realmente para inmigrantes
no es facil, es doble trabajo para
obtener "cosas facilo". Un inmigrante
se levanta muy temprano por la
mañana listo con su taza de
cafe para la jornada del dia.
Cortar yardas, limpiar casas,
trabajar en construcciones y mas
es lo que un inmigrante se dedica
hacer para llevar la comida

Figure 3. Sara's draft of her prologue in Spanish.

workshop model, or students' draft with revisions after one writing conference. This is Nayeli's initial, revised prologue draft completed during the second lesson.

> My mother always told me stories about how much her sister's life changed when she came with my grandfather and his wife to the United States twenty years ago. It was a difficult time for them because my grandfather was an old man and he didn't know if coming to the United States was the best for their lives. But a phrase changed everything when my mother's sister said "I will not stay in Cuba, I don't have a future here, I will leave with or without you all," she was only 13 years old.
>
> One day my mother told me we had the same opportunity as my aunt, to change everything, look for the success 90 miles away home. I cried the first time I heard those words, but my mother told me everything was about what I wanted. If leaving my grandmother was a good idea, I didn't want to even think about that terrible idea.
>
> But after a long time, that terrible idea became the best idea we had ever done. Now we are here in, the United States, building our

future, because I understand as my aunt, that I didn't have a bright future in Cuba, and I had to change that.

Now I'm thankful, excited and nervous about what is going to happen in my life, and I know it's the best idea just like my aunt's.

Reflection on and Analysis of the Lesson

Both the reading- and writing-focused portions of the lesson were successful, engaging the students with grade-level standards while also developing their L2 skills. The decision to use *The Distance Between Us* (Grande, 2012; Grande, 2017) ensured students were engaged with the text and the genre was relevant and inspiring. Students were excited to read a work by a person who they perceived to be like them and had a shared immigrant experience. Far too often, students become disengaged with literature in ELA classes because they have no connection with the author or the story (Rubin, 2014). Grande's memoir communicates to Seth's students that they can be authors and that their stories as immigrants are important. Though this selection is not part of the literary canon, it engaged students powerfully with the standards and empowered them to learn using culturally relevant literature that spoke to them. As writers, they saw that Latinos are celebrated authors and the stories they tell are worthy of being in print and shared with others. This affirmed the students, valuing their culture and their ability to author powerful stories that matter.

As the students utilized translanguaging to interact with the text and to write, Seth witnessed a depth and complexity present in their discussions and writings that was well beyond what they would have demonstrated in a purely monolingual setting where they would have had to repress many of their linguistic resources. They also spoke with him using both languages, facilitating deeper conversations about the text and more productive writing conferences. Instead of simple phrases such as "The author wanted us to know how she felt," students talked about how the author was demonstrating her sadness and isolation, and how this made the tone serious and the mood mournful. This kind of discussion allowed the students to demonstrate their proficiency as readers, and for teachers, peers, and staff to see them from an asset-based perspective instead of a deficit-based one.

Having some fluency in Spanish helped Seth greatly as students utilized translanguaging, allowing him to comprehend their speech and writing and to effectively communicate with them. For monolingual teachers, translanguaging is intimidating, and they might worry that students are not communicating about the content. However, there are many times when Seth's knowledge of Spanish is surpassed by his students, and he purposefully takes the stance of a language learner, asking them for help. In fact, prior to this lesson, Seth wrote an essay in Spanish, and he asked students to help him improve his L2 writing. It is important for emergent bilinguals to see their teachers as learners so that they will also take risks with their own learning. Like the research in the anchor article with translanguaging in an English-medium classroom (Daniel et al., 2017), these lessons illustrate that translanguaging can be a normal way to engage in effective literacy teaching. For all teachers, translanguaging does not have to be an intimidating concept, but it can be a pathway to provide more effective and powerful L2 instruction for high school students as they leverage all their languages to successfully engage in literacy.

Additional resources for this chapter are available at www.tesol.org/practices-highschool.

Seth M. Ross is an ESL, ELA, reading, and U.S. history high school teacher and a graduate student in reading education at Texas Woman's University, Denton, Texas, USA.

Mary Amanda Stewart is associate professor of reading education at Texas Woman's University, Denton, Texas, USA.

References

Au, K. H. (1998). Social constructivism and the school literacy learning of students of diverse backgrounds. *Journal of Literacy Research, 30*(2), 297–319.

Baker, C., & Wright, W. E. (2017). *Foundations of bilingual education and bilingualism* (6th ed.). Bristol, England: Multilingual Matters.

Cook, V. (2001). Using the first language in the classroom. *The Canadian Modern Language Review, 57*(3), 402–423.

Culham, R. (2014). *The writing thief: Using mentor texts to teach the craft of writing*. Newark, DE: International Reading Association.

Daniel, S. M., Jiménez, R. T., Pray, L., & Pacheco, M. B. (2017). Scaffolding to make translanguaging a classroom norm. *TESOL Journal*. Advance online publication. doi:10.1002/tesj.361

Dorner, L., M., Orellana, M., F., & Jiménez, R. (2008). "It's one of those things that you do to help the family." *Journal of Adolescent Research, 23*(5), 515–543.

Ebe, A. E., & Chapman-Santiago, C. (2016). Student voices shining through: Exploring translanguaging as a literary device. In O. García & T. Kleyn (Eds.), *Translanguaging with multilingual students: Learning from classroom moments* (pp. 57–82). New York, NY: Routledge.

García, O., Flores, N., & Chu, H. (2011). Extending bilingualism in U.S. secondary education: New variations. *International Multilingual Research Journal, 5*(1), 1–18.

García, O., Johnson, S. I., & Seltzer, K. (2017). *The translanguaging classroom: Leveraging student bilingualism for learning*. Philadelphia, PA: Caslon.

García, O., & Kleyn, T. (2016a). A translanguaging education policy: Disruptions and creating spaces of possibility. In O. García & T. Kleyn (Eds.), *Translanguaging with multilingual students: Learning from classroom moments*. (pp. 181–201). New York, NY: Routledge.

García, O., & Kleyn, T. (2016b). *Translanguaging with multilingual students: Learning from classroom moments*. New York, NY: Routledge.

García, O., & Menken, K. (2015). Cultivating an ecology of multilingualism in schools. In B. Spolsky, O. Inbar-Lourie, & M. Tannenbaum (Eds.), *Challenges for language education and policy: Making space for people* (pp. 95–108). New York, NY: Routledge.

García, O., & Wei, L. (2014). *Translanguaging: Language, bilingualism, and education*. New York, NY: Palgrave Pivot.

García-Mateus, S., & Palmer, D. (2017). Translanguaging pedagogies for positive identities in two-way dual language bilingual education. *Journal of Language, Identity & Education, 16*(4), 245–255.

Gort, M. (2006). Strategic codeswitching, interliteracy, and other phenomena of emergent bilingual writing: Lessons from first grade dual language classrooms. *Journal of Early Childhood Literacy, 6*(3), 323–354.

Grande, R. (2012). Prologue. In *The distance between us: A memoir* (pp. 3–4). New York, NY: Washington Square Press.

Grande, R. (2017). *The distance between us: Young readers education.* New York, NY: Simon & Schuster.

Hopewell, S. (2017). Pedagogies to challenge monolingual orientations to bilingual education in the United States. In B. Paulsrud, J. Rosén, B. Straszer, & Å. Wedin (Eds.), *New perspectives on translanguaging and education* (pp. 72–89). Bristol, England: Multilingual Matters.

Kittle, P. (2013). *Book love: Developing depth, stamina, and passion in adolescent readers.* Portsmouth, NH: Heinemann.

Leer, E. B., & Runck, B. C. (2016). Using writing workshops with English language learners. *English Journal, 105*(3), 107–109.

National Governors Association Center for Best Practices (NGA), & Council of Chief State School Officers (CCSSO). (2017). English language arts standards. Washington, DC: Author. Retrieved from http://www.corestandards.org/ELA-Literacy/

Orellana, M. F. (2009). *Translating childhoods: Immigrant youth, language, and culture.* New Brunswick, NJ: Rutgers University Press.

Rubin, D. I. (2014). Engaging Latino students in the secondary English classroom: A step toward breaking the school-to-prison pipeline. *Journal of Latinos and Education, 13*(3), 222–230.

Seltzer, K., Collins, B. A., & Angeles, K. M. (2016). Navigating turbulent waters: Translanguaging to support academic and socioemotional well-being. In O. García & T. Kleyn (Eds.), *Translanguaging with multilingual students: Learning from classroom moments* (pp. 149–159). New York, NY: Routledge.

Stewart, M. A., & Hansen-Thomas, H. (2016). Sanctioning a space for translanguaging in the secondary English class: A case of a transnational youth. *Research in the Teaching of English, 50*(4), 450–472.

Texas Education Code. Chapter 110. Texas Essential Knowledge and Skills for English Language Arts and Reading, Retrieved from http://ritter.tea.state.tx.us/rules/tac/chapter110/ch110c.html#110.30.

Texas Education Agency. (2011). ELPS-TELPAS proficiency level descriptors. Austin, TX: Author. Retrieved from https://tea.texas.gov/student.assessment/ell/telpas/

Tse, L. (1996). Language brokering in linguistic minority communities: The case of Chinese- and Vietnamese-American students. *Bilingual Research Journal, 20*(3–4), 485–498.

Williams, C. (1996). Secondary education: Teaching in the bilingual situation. In C. Williams, G. Lewis, & C. Baker (Eds.), *The language policy: Taking stock* (pp. 39–78). Llangefni, Wales: CAI.

World Class Instructional and Design and Assessment (WIDA). (2014). 2012 English language development standards. Retrieved from https://www.wida.us/standards/eld.aspx

Additional Resources

StoryCorps Oral Histories: storycorps.org/listen/

Translanguaging in Latino/a Literature: A CUNY-NYSIEB for Educators: www.cuny
-nysieb.org/wp-content/uploads/2016/05/CUNY-NYSIEB-Latino-Literature
-Guide-Final-January-2015.pdf

Translanguaging in Curriculum and Instruction: A CUNY-NYSIEB Guide for
Educators: www.cuny-nysieb.org/wp-content/uploads/2016/05/Translanguaging
-Guide-Curr-Inst-Final-December-2014.pdf

Translanguaging Pedagogy For Writing: A CUNY-NYSIEB Guide for Educators:
www.cuny-nysieb.org/wp-content/uploads/2016/05/TLG-Pedagogy-Writing
-04-15-16.pdf

Teaching Bilinguals (Even if You're Not One): A CUNY-NYSIEB Webseries
(Episode 4 is especially relevant as an ELA teacher teaches literature in her
multilingual classroom.): www.cuny-nysieb.org/teaching-bilinguals-webseries/

Suggestions for Memoirs to Use as Mentor Texts

Arce, J. (2016). *My (underground) American dream: My true story as an undocumented immigrant who became a Wall Street executive.* New York, NY: Hatchet Book Group.

Beah, I. (2007). *A long way gone: Memoirs of a boy soldier* (1st ed.). New York, NY: Farrar, Straus and Giroux.

Bell, C., & Lasky, D. (2014). *El Deafo.* New York, NY: Amulet Books.

Beyer, R. (2013). *Little fish: A memoir from a different kind of year.* San Francisco, CA: Zest Books.

Brierley, S. (2013). *A long way home: A memoir.* New York, NY: Penguin Random House.

Calcaterra, R. (2013). *Etched in sand: A true story of five siblings who survived an unspeakable childhood on Long Island.* New York, NY: HarperCollins.

Chen, J. (2008). *Mao and me.* New York, NY: Enchanted Lion Books.

Chikwanine, M., & Humphreys, J. D. (2015). *Child soldier: When boys and girls are used in war.* Toronto, Canada: Citizen Can Press.

Dumas, F. (2003). *Funny in Farsi.* New York, NY: Random House.

Eig, J. (2017). *Ali: A life.* New York, NY: Houghton Mifflin Harcourt.

Gantos, J. (2002). *Hole in my life* (1st ed.). New York, NY: Farrar, Straus and Giroux.

Grealy, L. (2016). *Autobiography of a face.* New York, NY: Houghton Mifflin Harcourt.

Hernandez, D., & Rubin, S. G. (2013). *They call me a hero: A memoir of my youth* (1st ed.). New York, NY: Simon & Schuster Books for Young Readers.

Hernandez, D., Rubin, S. G., & Verdecia, C. (2013). *Me llaman héroe: Recuerdos de mi juventud.* New York, NY: Simon & Schuster Books for Young Readers.

Kuo, M. (2017). *Reading with Patrick: A teacher, a student, and a life-changing friendship.* New York, NY: HarperCollins.

Lee, H. (2016) *The girl with seven names: Escape from North Korea.* London, England: HarperCollins.

Lythcott-Haims, J. (2017). *Real American: A memoir.* New York, NY: Henry Holt.

Marin, G. R. (2009). *My Papa Diego and me: Memories of my father and his art.* San Francisco, CA: Children's Book Press.

Martinez, A. (2016). *My voice: A memoir.* New York, NY: Penguin Random House.

Melvin, L. (2017). *Chasing space: An astronaut's story of grit, grace, and second chances.* New York, NY: HarperCollins.

McMullan, J. (2014). *Leaving China: An artist paints his World War II childhood.* Chapel Hill, NC: Algonquin.

Mochizuki, K. (1997). *Passage to freedom: The Sugihara story.* New York, NY: Lee & Low Books.

Nivola, C. A. (2011). *Orani: My father's village.* New York, NY: Farrar, Straus and Giroux.

Pantoja, A. (2002). *Memoir of a visionary: Antonia Pantoja (Hispanic Civil Rights series.)* Houston, TX: Arte Público Press.

Polacco, P. (1998). *Thank you, Mr. Falker.* New York: Philomel Books.

Say, A. (2011). *Drawing from Memory.* New York: Scholastic Press.

Shulevitz, U. (2008). *How I learned geography.* New York, NY: Farrar Straus Giroux.

Sis, P. (2007). The wall: Growing up behind the Iron Curtain. New York, NY: Farrar, Straus and Giroux.

Skrypuch, M. F., & Ho, T. (2016). *Adrift at sea: A Vietnamese boy's story of survival.* Toronto, Canada: Pajama Press.

Thomas, L. (2007). *Turning white: A memoir of change.* Toronto, Canada: Momentum Books.

Troncoso, S. (2011). *Crossing borders: Personal essays.* Houston: TX: Arte Público Press.

Verghese, A. (2016). *When breath becomes air.* New York, NY: Random House.

Willard Schultz, J. (2017). *My life as an Indian: The story of a red woman and a white man in the lodges of the Blackfeet.* Arcadia Press.

Yousafzai, M. (2013). *I am Malala: The girl who stood up for education and was shot by the Taliban.* London, England: Orion.

Section 2

Social Studies

Breaking Through: Using Authentic Literature to Teach Social Studies

Jacqueline Riley, Patsy Sosa-Sánchez

Introduction

Meeting the academic and linguistic needs of K–12 English learners (ELs) can be a challenging task. To learn how to best serve ELs, many educators receive Sheltered Instruction Observation Protocol (SIOP) model training. SIOP is a research-based model that consists of eight components: preparation, building background, comprehensible input, strategies, interaction, practice and application, lesson delivery, and evaluation and assessment (Echevarría, Vogt, & Short, 2008). The teacher's integration of each component in any content area allows students to simultaneously develop language and academic content.

To demonstrate the positive impact SIOP training can have on EL instruction, this chapter focuses on the lessons of one SIOP-trained social studies teacher. For the past 7 years, the featured teacher, Lee, attended three to four district-led SIOP workshops each year. We explain how he successfully implemented a multiday SIOP lesson on immigration. He taught the lesson to his 11th-grade U.S. History class, which included ELs and non-ELs, where approximately 31% of his students were Hispanic. Of the 23 students in this course, 10 were identified as ELs and 13 were not. The 13 non-ELs included students who were formerly ELs but who were redesignated to English proficient, and native English speakers. In this chapter, we highlight the ELs' responses to the SIOP strategies provided.

Synopsis of Original Research

Short, D. J., Fidelman, C. G., & Louguit, M. (2012). Developing academic language in English language learners through sheltered instruction. *TESOL Quarterly, 46*, 334–361. doi:10.1002/tesq.20

Short, Fidelman, and Louguit (2012) compared the reading, writing, and oral language IDEA Language Proficiency Test (IPT) of middle and high school students whose teachers had and had not received SIOP model training. The researchers employed a quasi-experimental design in which two northern New Jersey (USA) districts were matched as closely as possible based on a variety of factors. One high school and two middle schools from each district participated in the study. One district served as the SIOP intervention group and the other served as the comparison group. Teacher participants included both volunteers and teachers assigned to the study. Teachers in the SIOP intervention group received the following professional development: (1) Summer institutes and workshops, (2) school-based coachings and observations, and (3) technical support. In contrast, teachers in the comparison group participated in regular professional development and did not receive SIOP model training. After the trainings, a majority (56% for Year 1 and 71% for Year 2) of teachers that participated in the SIOP interventions were high SIOP model implementers versus a minority (5% for Year 1 and 17% of Year 2) of teachers in the comparison group.

Additionally, IPT scores were collected at the beginning of the study, during Year 1 and during Year 2. The researchers found that during Years 1 and 2, students of SIOP model–trained teachers outperformed the comparison group on writing and oral language as assessed by the IPT. By the second year, the performance of students whose teachers had received the SIOP intervention scored statistically significantly higher than students in the comparison group in all three areas (reading, writing, and oral language). Based on this data, Short et al. (2012) concluded that the use of SIOP model instruction, when used with fidelity, improves student performance. Their findings highlight the benefits of providing SIOP model training for all teachers.

Rationale

SIOP model training helps educators understand and apply best practice for teaching ELs (Daniel & Conlin, 2015; DelliCarpini, 2008; Echevarría & Short, 2011; Echevarría, Short, & Powers, 2008; Pray & Monhardt, 2009; Short, Echevarría, & Richards-Tutor, 2011; Short et al., 2012). Each of the eight components of the SIOP model has been tested in multiple content areas and across all grade levels. Furthermore, the results have been independently supported by empirical studies (Short & Echevarría, 1999). Following, we summarize each of the eight components that compose the SIOP model as outlined in *Making Content Comprehensible for English Learners: The SIOP Model* (Echevarría, Vogt, & Short, 2008).

The SIOP model begins with component one, preparation, in which the teacher creates a lesson plan based on clear content and language objectives. These objectives are defined, displayed, repeated, and reviewed throughout the lesson. Each activity in the lesson helps to achieve these objectives. During the preparation phase, the teacher selects concepts that are appropriate for students' age and abilities. Further planning is necessary to adapt the content to a range of students' proficiency levels. The teacher also carefully considers what supplementary materials (e.g., visuals, multimedia, manipulatives) will be used to promote comprehension. Throughout the lesson, purposefully selected materials are used to meet the linguistic and academic needs of students. The lesson is designed to provide opportunities for students to read, write, listen, and speak.

The second component, building background, requires that the teacher explicitly link the material presented to students' prior knowledge, experiences, and past learning. In context of the lesson, academic vocabulary is written, repeated, and highlighted. The third component, comprehensible input, mandates that speech is suitable for students' proficiency levels and academic tasks are clearly explained. The teacher presents the material in a variety of ways and allows students the opportunity to demonstrate their learning through different tasks.

The fourth component, strategies, requires that students are provided with many opportunities to use learning strategies to support comprehension. To promote strategy use, students use higher order thinking skills as they answer questions and complete tasks. As students participate in the lesson, they receive adequate scaffolding to facilitate comprehension.

The fifth component, interaction, includes repeated opportunities for the teacher and students to discuss the topics presented. Students are provided with appropriate wait time and encouraged to elaborate on their responses. Learners have frequent opportunities to clarify concepts using their first language, texts in their native language, a peer/aid, and other resources. Moreover, the teacher groups students in ways that support the lesson's language and content objectives.

The sixth component, practice and application, enables students to utilize hands-on learning material to practice and apply new content and language knowledge. Students participate in a variety of activities, which encompass each of the four language domains (reading, writing, listening, and speaking).

Through lesson delivery, the seventh component, the teacher implements a lesson that supports both the content and language objectives. Students are engaged 90–100% of the time in a lesson that is appropriate for their abilities. As part of the eighth component, evaluation and assessment, students review key vocabulary and concepts. Finally, throughout the lesson, students receive regular feedback from the teacher and peers regarding their content and language performance.

Lesson Plan

Based on Short et al.'s (2012) article, we created an 8-day 11th-grade social studies lesson to demonstrate each of the components of a successful SIOP model unit. The lesson's activities allow students to build on their background knowledge, practice new vocabulary, and think critically about the evolution of Mexican immigration into the United States. The lesson incorporates SIOP model strategies to be used prior to, during, and after reading Francisco Jiménez's *Breaking Through* (2001).

Breaking Through was selected because it focuses on immigration, a timely and relatable topic for many ELs. Furthermore, the theme fits with the class's curriculum, beginning prior to World War II and ending with the Civil Rights Movements. In this autobiographical work, Jiménez tells of his family's experience immigrating to the United States from Mexico during the 1950s. As economic challenges arise, the family struggles to stay together, and some family members are eventually forced to return to Mexico. The book includes 25 chapters; however, we realize that teachers may have limited time to dedicate to an individual unit. Therefore, our 8-day lesson plan focuses on just the first eight chapters.

Lesson Plan Title	Mexican Immigration: Then and Now
Grade/Subject Area	Grade 11; U.S. history
Duration	8 (50-minute) class periods
Proficiency Levels	WIDA (2014): Levels 4–6 (Expanding to Reaching)
Content and Language Objectives	Students will be able to • create graphic representations of how migrant workers contribute to and shape the culture of the United States as depicted in *Breaking Through*. (Content) • synthesize information collected from lesson activities to write a position paper. (Content) • demonstrate comprehension of content vocabulary through class discussion and completion of graphic organizers. (Language) • discuss both opinions and personal experiences, as well as video and written resources surrounding immigration. (Language)
Alignment to Standards	**Common Core State Standards** (CCSS; NGA & CCSSO, 2010) • *CCSS.ELA-LITERACY.W.11-12.1*: Write arguments to support claims in an analysis of substantive topics or texts, using valid reasoning and relevant and sufficient evidence: (B) Develop claim(s) and counterclaims fairly and thoroughly, supplying the most relevant evidence for each while pointing out the strengths and limitations of both in a manner that anticipates the audience's knowledge level, concerns, values, and possible biases.

(continued on next page)

Lesson Plan *(continued)*	
Alignment to Standards *(continued)*	• *CCSS.ELA-LITERACY.W.11-12.8:* Gather relevant information from multiple authoritative print and digital sources, using advanced searches effectively; assess the strengths and limitations of each source in terms of the task, purpose, and audience; integrate information into the text selectively to maintain the flow of ideas, avoiding plagiarism and overreliance on any one source and following a standard format for citation. **WIDA English Language Proficiency Standards** (2014) • *Listening (Level 5: Bridging):* Evaluate the appropriateness of messages or information from a variety of sources. • *Speaking (Level 4: Expanding):* Discuss pros and cons of plays, films, stories, books, songs, poems, computer programs, or magazine articles. • *Reading (Level 5: Bridging):* Revise thoughts and conclusions based on information from text. • *Writing (Level 5: Bridging):* Expand and elaborate written language as directed.
Outcomes	Students will • conduct an interview with an immigrant who resides within their community to gain personal insight into the life and contributions of immigrants to American culture. • write a position paper on immigration using graphic organizers and data supporting their opinions about Mexican immigration to the United States. • read about Mexican immigrants from *Breaking Through* and other online supplemental sources. • listen to a variety of sources including video, classmates and other immigrants.
Materials	• *Breaking Through* (Jiménez, 2001) class set • Content area journal • Computers • Document camera • Projector • Chart paper • Appendixes A and B (available on the companion website for this book) — Position papers sample (Appendix A) — Interview question guide (Appendix B)

Highlighted Teaching Strategies

The multiday SIOP model lesson plan presented here contains the following strategies for social studies and literacy:

- Carefully written content and language objectives (Echevarría, Vogt, & Short, 2008)
- Four-corners vocabulary (Vogt & Echevarría, 2008)
- Framed outlines (Vogt & Echevarría,2008)
- Split-page note-taking (Vogt & Echevarría, 2008)
- Inside outside circle (Kagan, 1989)
- Go graphic (Venn Diagram; Vogt & Echevarría, 2008)
- Stop the DVD (Vogt & Echevarría, 2008)
- Take your corners (Kagan, 1989)

Note that some previously developed strategies have been integrated to achieve different components of the SIOP model.

Procedures
Day 1

SIOP Component 1: Preparation

SIOP Strategy: Carefully written content and language objectives

The lesson begins with writing carefully planned lesson objectives on the board (Echevarría, Vogt, & Short, 2008). To help introduce the language and content objectives, start with Take Your Corner. Place a large sheet of paper containing each of the following statements in a different corner of the classroom:

1. If I lived in Mexico with my family and didn't have food or money, I would stay in Mexico with my family.

2. If I lived in Mexico with my family and didn't have food or money, I would come to the United States and send money back to my family.

3. If I lived in Mexico with my family and didn't have food or money, I would bring my family with me to the United States.

4. If I lived in Mexico with my family and didn't have food or money, I would alternate between working in Mexico and the United States.

Ask students to stand next to the statement with which they most closely agree. Then, have them explain why they chose their respective statements and offer any options not listed. Following the discussion, introduce the book *Breaking Through* and show a video book trailer (Pust, 2017; access at www.youtube.com/watch?v =8tf9xS1V2gY or link directly from the companion website for this book). This helps students to better anticipate what they will read.

SIOP Component 2: Building background

SIOP Strategy: Four-corners vocabulary (see Figure 1)

Prior to reading the book, introduce the following key vocabulary words related to the novel:

- Immigration visa
- Desegregation
- La Migra
- Deportation
- Bracero
- Sharecropper
- Barracks

As each word is presented, show realia or a printed image to represent the word and ask students where they have heard the word used before. In groups of four to five students, have them portray one of the words using four-corner vocabulary graphic organizers. Four corners (Vogt & Echevarría, 2008) requires students to illustrate, write a sentence, define, and write the given vocabulary word. As students work to complete their four-corners assignment, they may use their phones, computers, and books to find additional information. Once each group has completed their graphic organizer, they share their work with their classmates.

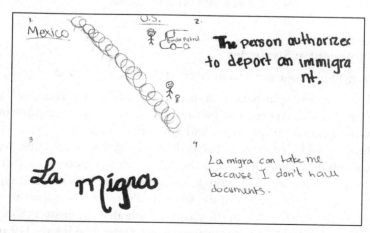

Figure 1. Veronica and Maria's four-corner vocabulary.

Day 2

SIOP Component 3: Comprehensible input

SIOP Strategy: Framed outline (see Figure 2)

Read Chapter 1 of *Breaking Through* aloud as students complete the framed outline (Vogt & Echevarría, 2008), which summarizes the text but omits key information. For example, "Francisco felt comfortable around Mr. Ostereen because . . ." Students are responsible for filling in the missing information. In doing so, they are forced to monitor their comprehension of the text and summarize what they have heard.

Francisco was constantly afraid between the ages of four and fourteen of
...... because... *He was scared to get caught by la migra.*

The main reason Francisco did not want to return to Mexico was because
..... *He did not want to return to Mexico because he liked going to school.*

When Francisco was picked up at school by immigration officials, the
situation is ironic because.... *Him and his family didn't tell anyone they were undocumented.*

After reaching the immigration office, the family travels back to Mexico by
way of ...... *Bus.*

In the story, Francisco takes a rock from the motel office and then returns
it. The author's purpose to describe the character is ...
When the family is granted an immigrant visa, it is good news because ...
He knew taking things that don't belong to you is bad. It was a good thing, because now him and his family can be in the U.S. and work legally.

Roberto, a high school student, and Francisco, a middle school student,
are sent back to Santa Maria to live and work by themselves. This situation
can be good/bad because...
This can be good because their going to earn money with no fear of getting deported and bad because their far away from his family + they are going to be on their own.

When they are boarding the bus, Francisco cries when he sees a little boy
on his father's lap because... *He wishes he was with dad and family.*

Figure 2. Gloria's framed outline.

Day 3

SIOP Component 4: Strategies

SIOP Strategy: Split-page note-taking (see Table 1)

Model how to use split-page note-taking (Vogt & Echevarría, 2008) with the class. Explain that this strategy can be used as another way to monitor one's comprehension by generating questions and answering those questions. Then, show students how to fold a piece of paper in half to create two columns. Model how to label one column "Questions" and the other column "Answers." Read the first paragraph of Chapter 2 aloud. As you do so, demonstrate how to write a question in the first column and the answer in the second column. Ask students to think of at least 10 questions as they listen to the chapter. Note that the answers to some questions are stated in the text, but the answers to others must be inferred or may not be

Table 1. Teacher's Sample of Split-Page Notes

Questions	Answers
1. What is a bedpan?	A small, portable container used to dispose waste
2. Why was it important to empty the bedpan daily?	To dump bodily waste

answered at all. Ask students to put a star next to questions that could be debated, and later, write that question on a Post-it note to share with the class.

Day 4

SIOP Component 5: Interaction

SIOP Strategy: Inside outside circle

Begin reading Chapter 3 of *Breaking Through* aloud. Next, ask students to share the discussion questions they wrote on their Post-it notes during the previous class. Have the students put the their notes on the board. Select the questions that will be used during inside outside circle (Kagan, 1989), and write these questions on the board. In inside outside circle, students form two concentric circles; each person in the outside circle faces their partner in the inside circle. Students have 2 minutes to discuss their responses to the first question. When you signal time is up, students in the outside circle rotate one student to the right. Once everyone is facing a new partner, they discuss the next question. This continues until students have answered all questions presented by the teacher.

Day 5

SIOP Component 6: Practice and application

SIOP Strategy: Go graphic (Venn diagram; see Figure 3)

Begin the lesson by reading Chapter 4 of *Breaking Through* aloud. Working in pairs, students take notes on and synthesize the information from the book and websites related to immigration. Inform students that they will be looking specifically for information related to how political, social, and economic needs resulted in increases and decreases in Mexicans' immigration into the United States in the 1950s and today. Decide if students will be provided with the websites or if they will select their own. If students are asked to find their own websites, first discuss what types of information they will search for and how to identify credible websites which contain accurate information. Before students search the internet independently, model the internet search process, pointing out which key terms you used and how you decided if the websites reviewed contained reliable information.

Next, have the students create a Venn diagram (Vogt & Echevarría, 2008) comparing immigration in the 1950s to immigration today. Using their notes, have students discuss with one another what they noticed, particularly any patterns in the nation's political, social, and economic needs.

Conclude the lesson with a discussion of what students wrote on their Venn diagrams. During this time, highlight the changes in immigration patterns over time. To help focus students on the historical changes, pose the following questions: Why was it so important for Francisco's family to return peacefully to Mexicali in the 1950s? What was the difference in amnesty periods for immigration in the 1950s versus today? What might happen if Francisco and his family chose not to return to Mexicali in this day and age?

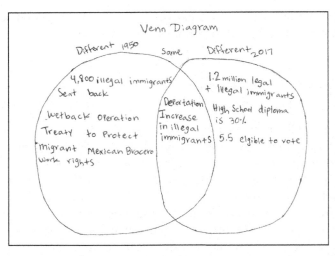

Figure 3. Yolanda's Venn diagram.

Day 6

SIOP Component 7: Lesson delivery

SIOP Strategy: Stop the DVD

Using the stop the DVD strategy (Vogt & Echevarría, 2008), share selected videos about immigration. Each of the videos (see Additional Resources or link directly from the companion website for this book) shows testimonies and real stories of families who have experienced immigration struggles similar to the main character, Francisco, in *Breaking Through*. Help students to make the connection between the families in the videos and those in the book.

In students' social studies journals, have them create a T-chart (see Figure 4), in which they title one column "I wonder" and the other "I see." Stop the YouTube videos at important points and ask students what they're thinking, giving them time to fill in the "I wonder" column with questions they have. As students watch the video, they should write answers to their questions in the "I see" column. After completing the T-chart, the class discusses what they wrote and any unanswered questions.

Day 7

SIOP Components 7/8: Lesson delivery; review and assessment

SIOP strategy: Take your corners

Repeat the activity done on the first day of the unit in which students were asked to go to the corner with the statement that best represented their response to the following question: "If I lived in Mexico with my family and didn't have food or money, I would . . ." Have students discuss whether their opinions have changed since the beginning of the unit and why or why not.

According to the SIOP model, take your corners (Kagan, 2009) is classified under lesson delivery. However, in this lesson, you can also use it to review. As students

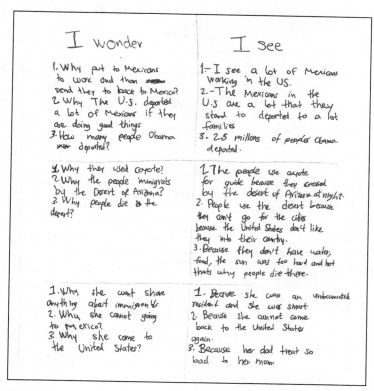

I wonder	I see
1. Why put to Mexicans to work and than send they to back to Mexico?	1.- I see a lot of Mexicans working in the US.
2. Why The U.S. deported a lot of Mexicans if they are doing good things	2.- The Mexicans in the U.S are a lot that they stand to deported to a lot families
3. How many people Obama was deported?	3.- 2.5 millons of people Obama deported.
1. Why they used coyote?	1. The people use coyote for guide because they crossed by the desert of Arizona at night.
2. Why the people immigrats by the Desert of Arizona?	2. People use the desert because they can't go for the cities because the United States don't like they into their country.
3. Why people die to the desert?	3. Because they don't have water, food, the sun was too hard and hot thats why people die there.
1. Why she wont share anything about immigrants	1. Beause she was an undocumented resident and she was short
2. Why she cannot going to mexico?	2. Beause she cannot come back to the United States again.
3. Why she come to the United States?	3. Because her dad treat so bad to her mom.

Figure 4. Juan's T-chart.

explain their choice, they tie in information and academic vocabulary presented earlier in the unit. Thus, rather than relying on opinions and experiences alone, students synthesize the materials presented throughout the unit to support their positions.

Closing

As a whole group, students respond to the following higher order thinking questions. As there are no right and no wrong answers, it is a way to encourage further discussion.

- What do you suppose Francisco Jiménez is trying to highlight about the lives of some immigrant families?

- Why do you suppose he titled this piece *Breaking Through*?

Additionally, assign students an "immigrant interview" (see Figure 5) and position paper (see Appendix A): The students conduct an interview with an immigrant in their community and bring the interview with them to class on Day 8 of the unit. Remind students that they do not have to include the interviewees' names and that the information will not be shared outside of the class. Utilizing the Interview Question Guide (Appendix B), each student should use their data to write a position paper on immigration.

Immigrant Interview

1. Name of person being interviewed: _Alvaro_

2. Relationship: _Dad_

3. How did you conduct this interview? (circle one)

   (In person)   By telephone   By email

4. Where did you move from and to where? _Muzquiz, Coahuila_ (from) _Denton, Tx_ (to)

5. Why did you move? _To find a better life, dad recently died, and follow the "American Dream."_

6. Did you make this move alone? _____ Yes ___✓___ No

7. If "yes", how did it affect your relationship with your family? If "no", who made this move with you?

   With other family members and the "coyote."

8. Was it your family that you moved with? ___✓___ Yes _____ No

9. Do you feel your family was affected by this move? If so, how? What were some of the changes you encounter by this move into a new country or location?

   Yes because I was the youngest and left my mother with my older siblings.

10. Do you feel there were any benefits in your decision to move?

    Yes I got married had 3 children and have had a job for 20 years.

11. Is there anything else you would like us to know about your moving experience? (Write notes on the back side of this sheet).

https://drive.google.com/drive/u/1/folders/1eGmD8EKhchxFsTyQqQfzVAh_px9hWojD   1/1

Figure 5. Yolanda's immigrant interview.

Extensions

The multiday lesson can be extended in a variety of ways. For instance, you could incorporate the economic effects and policies surrounding past and present immigration. You may wish to present the topic of immigration in context of a given time period (e.g., the Industrial Revolution) to provide a more complete picture of immigrants' motives for coming to the United States. The activities presented in this lesson could also be used as the basis for fiction and nonfiction narratives in which students write about their own experiences related to immigration or what it might be like to be an immigrant.

Caveats

Many of the students in Lee's classroom related to Francisco Jiménez's experience crossing the Rio Grande and living in Texas. However, nonimmigrants and those who have immigrated in other ways, from other parts of the world and to other parts of the United States, may not make these same connections.

Assessment and Evaluation

After the students have discussed the higher order thinking questions from the Closing, they share their findings from their interviews. Students take notes as they listen to their classmates' interview findings. These notes, the material presented in the unit, and their own experiences serve as the basis for their position papers. Assess the final paper for both language and content.

Reflection on and Analysis of the Lesson

This multiday lesson was based on Short et al.'s (2012) research which suggested that students of SIOP model–trained teachers will outperform students of teachers who have not received SIOP model training. In Lee's class, he taught a multiday lesson on immigration in which he successfully incorporated each of the eight components of the SIOP model. In doing so, he provided ample opportunities for students to connect to their background knowledge, presented the content and language in a comprehensible manner, allowed students to practice using the academic vocabulary presented in context, and assessed students using a variety of methods.

First, the lesson connected social studies content to students' lives. By building on students' background knowledge, the material (in this case immigration) was made meaningful to them. Through activities like inside outside circle and the immigrant interview, many ELs shared their own experience of being an immigrant themselves and/or experiences surrounding the immigrants they knew. As students completed the four-corners vocabulary graphic organizer, they also relied on their background knowledge. For instance, in Figure 1, the students wrote a sentence in which they incorporated the word *deported* to describe what could happen to them and their families.

Furthermore, after each lesson, students made connections to the content, and some discussed challenges they faced when immigrating to the United States. For example, they experienced a lot of fear: fear of drowning in the river, fear of being caught by U.S. Immigration and Customs Enforcement, and fear of being separated from their families in the process of getting to their assigned coyote (one who smuggles immigrants into the United States). A sense of appreciation for their lives today and gratitude for what their parents had given them was evident in the conversations.

Second, Lee provided students with comprehensible input. The lesson incorporated a variety of scaffolds to promote the development of the English language and academic content. framed outlines, Venn diagrams, split-page notes, and T-charts proved to be useful tools in scaffolding both content and language. These resources helped students to focus on key information while providing supports to assist them in expressing their thoughts and analyzing information. Lee also utilized scaffolding as he presented visual supports, such as video and differentiated questions, based on students' proficiency levels.

Third, the teacher embedded within the lesson multiple opportunities for students to use academic vocabulary in context. Key words were presented and highlighted in the book, in the videos, in other resources, and through class discussion. The new vocabulary was further reinforced as students completed their four-corners vocabulary assignment and wrote a position paper explaining their views on immigration.

Finally, through varied formal and informal assessments, students demonstrated English and social studies content in different ways. The nature of the assignments and scaffolds allowed students, regardless of proficiency level, to actively participate. For instance, through the four-corners vocabulary assignment, students showed their understanding of new vocabulary words by not only defining them but also illustrating the words. Thus, even if students were unable to express themselves through writing, their drawings could be used to check their understanding of the vocabulary.

The multiday immigration lesson was inspired by Short et al.'s (2012) research and offers an example of what a SIOP model–lesson plan might include. Short et al. noted quantitative gains in students' IPT reading, writing, and oral language scores; we observed our own, different successes in the form of students connecting the content to their background knowledge, increases in student comprehension, increased opportunities for students to use academic vocabulary in context, and students being able to demonstrate their learning through a variety of assessments.

The appendixes for this chapter are available at www.tesol.org/practices-highschool.

Jacqueline Riley is an assistant professor in the Department of Curriculum and Instruction at Texas A&M University at Commerce, Texas, USA.

Patsy Sosa-Sánchez is assistant professor at the University of North Texas at Dallas, USA.

References

Daniel, S. M., & Conlin, L. (2015). Shifting attention back to students within the Sheltered Instruction Observation Protocol. *TESOL Quarterly, 49*, 169–187.

DelliCarpini, M. (2008). Success with ELLs: Working with English language learners: Looking back, moving forward. *The English Journal, 98*(1), 98–101.

Echevarría, J., & Short, D. J. (2011). *The SIOP model: A professional development framework for a comprehensive school-wide intervention*. CREATE Brief. Washington, DC: CREDE Center for Applied Linguistics.

Echevarría, J., Short, D., & Powers, K. (2008). Making content comprehensible for non-native speakers of English: The SIOP model. *International Journal of Learning, 14*(11), 41–49.

Echevarría, J., Vogt, M., & Short, D. (2016). *Making content comprehensible for English learners: The SIOP model*. New York, NY: Pearson.

Jiménez, F. (2002). *Breaking through*. New York, NY: Houghton Mifflin Harcourt.

Kagan, S. (1989). The structural approach to cooperative learning. *Educational Leadership, 47*(4), 12–15.

National Governors Association Center for Best Practices (NGA), & Council of Chief State School Officers (CCSSO). (2010). English language arts standards. Washington, DC: Author. Retrieved from http://www.corestandards.org/ELA-Literacy/

Pray, L., & Monhardt, R. (2009). Sheltered instruction techniques for ELLs. *Science and children, 46*(7), 34–38.

Short, D. J., & Echevarría, J. (1999). *The sheltered instruction observation protocol: A tool for teacher-research collaboration and professional development. Educational Practice Report 3.* Washington, DC: CREDE Center for Applied Linguistics.

Short, D. J., Echevarría, J., & Richards-Tutor, C. (2011). Research on academic literacy development in sheltered instruction classrooms. *Language Teaching Research, 15*(3), 363–380.

Short, D. J., Fidelman, C. G., & Louguit, M. (2012). Developing academic language in English language learners through sheltered instruction. *TESOL Quarterly, 46,* 334–361. doi:10.1002/tesq.20

Vogt, M., & Echevarría, J. (2008). *99 ideas and activities for teaching English learners with the SIOP model.* Boston, MA: Pearson Allyn and Bacon.

World Class Instructional and Design and Assessment. (2014). WIDA's 2012 amplification of the English Language Development Standards, kindergarten–grade 12.

Additional Resources

Immigration of the 1950s. (2012, February 12). Retrieved from https://1950immigration.wordpress.com/

Mexican Immigration Timeline: https://www.youtube.com/watch?v=Q7PUnuTh5tM

Pust, D. (2017, May 9). *Breaking through by Francisco Jimenez.* Retrieved from https://www.youtube.com/watch?v=8tf9xS1V2gY

Should we stop or help those who come to the U.S. illegally?: https://www.youtube.com/watch?v=1eMq-MTw2wA

Undocumented valedictorian: https://www.youtube.com/watch?v=lcVGTfRSHj8

5

Picture This! Using Illustrated Books to Support Comprehension of Social Studies Complex Texts

Tamra Dollar, Patricia Flint, Holly Hansen-Thomas

Introduction

High school teachers often feel the overwhelming pressure to teach grade-level standards to English learners (ELs), but they do not have sufficient access to informational texts or teaching strategies to make content accessible to students. Language barriers between teachers and ELs further complicate teachers' efforts to teach the required standards. This chapter is rooted in Palincsar and Schleppegrell's (2014) article entitled "Focusing on Language and Meaning While Learning With Text," which addressed ways to ensure that complex, informational texts have a presence in the curriculum. Based on this article, the lesson highlighted in this chapter implements the use of a children's autobiographical book as a comprehension strategy to help identify the cause and effect relationships of World War II (WWII).

The lesson was carried out in a high school classroom over two class periods designed to address Social Studies Texas Essential Knowledge and Skills (2018) and Common Core State Standards (CCSS; 2017), as well as the Texas English Language Proficiency Standards (ELPS). Participants were ELs in Grades 9–12 with English language proficiency ratings from beginner to advanced based on a four-point scale of beginner to advanced high. High school social studies standards were selected that targeted the major events and issues of WWII and included academic vocabulary and text analysis.

The teacher-researchers, Tamra (first author) and Patricia (second author), are two White monolingual-English-speaking doctoral students working on a federally funded grant led in part by Holly (third author), who participated in the lesson described in this chapter as a participant observer. ELLevate! is a US$2.1 million professional development grant project that supports more than 300 faculty members, administrators and professional support staff in two high schools located in a medium-sized community in north Texas.[1] ELLevate! takes a whole-school reform approach to implement a four-tier professional development project on three areas that are key when instructing adolescent ELs: language, literacy, and engagement. Through the ELLevate! grant, the teacher-researchers worked with ELs in one of the participating schools by offering a summer literacy institute focused on vocabulary development, oral and written language acquisition, and comprehension using a variety of texts. The students, eight females and one male, were between the ages of 16 and 18 years old and had been in the United States anywhere from 2 months to 8 years. They came from countries including Mexico, Venezuela, and Honduras. The students' first language was Spanish, and most had been schooled in Spanish rather than English. At the end of the summer, the students asked the teachers to return in the fall for an after-school book club. A weekly book club was established using student-selected books, provided by the grant in English and Spanish. Some of the books were fiction, and others were historical nonfiction, such as the one described in this chapter.

Synopsis of Original Research

Palincsar, A. S., & Schleppegrell, M. J. (2014). Focusing on language and meaning while learning with text. *TESOL Quarterly, 48*, 616–623. doi:10.1002/tesq.178

In their 2014 article, Palincsar and Schleppegrell theorized that focusing on language and meaning, or metalanguage, through the use of informational texts, will facilitate elementary level ELs' learning. According to Schleppegrell (2013), "Metalanguage refers to language about language and includes both using terminology to refer to language as well as engaging in talk about language and meaning" (p. 616). Metalanguage strategies for supporting ELs accessing information from text include graphic organizers, building prior knowledge and vocabulary instruction, and fueling students' interests and motivation. Language used on a conversational level adds meaning in a text because word choice can help or hinder understanding. Palincsar and Schleppegrell worked on developing strategies that aid teachers in working with ELs regarding how the structure of the English language works in the texts they will encounter in school.

The sociocultural language theories of Vygotsky (1986) and Halliday (1978) informed Palincsar and Schleppegrell's (2014) work. Specifically, the theories that children learn by interacting with others, which in turn allows them to learn language, were those that played the most salient roles. The authors' perspective is consistent with research that second language development can be built through correspondence with and evaluation of meaningful texts. The assumption that second language teaching needs to take into account a student's cognitive level and

---

[1] This material is based on work supported by the U.S. Department of Education's Office of English Acquisition under Award No. CFDA 84.365Z. T365Z160017. Among other items, the grant funds were used to purchase iPads to provide students with a digital literacy experience.

consider the use of state and district standards and grade-level texts was underscored, as well as the notion that scaffolding the use of complex texts can support second language acquisition. Some examples provided in the article included how teachers and students working together on shared activities can facilitate meaning derivation from texts, and teachers using visuals and video can assist student understanding of texts.

Part of the research in the article (Palincsar & Schleppegrell, 2014) described how the authors developed curriculum to facilitate children's reading comprehension of science texts so that the students could produce written arguments supported with text evidence. Palincsar and Schleppegrell gave an example from their curriculum that teaches, using science texts, the meaning of content vocabulary through the use of reading and writing. This curriculum aided teachers in implementing learning-focused strategies to help students defend a position while using text evidence to support their claim. Multiple science texts were used to support a claim on content vocabulary meaning. In a brief mini-lesson on the science language feature *likelihood*, students found words in the texts that explained what they understood about a chosen language feature of science that is pertinent to reading and writing and added them to a graphic organizer. Students also engaged in small-group conversations prior to writing about the texts to help solidify their understanding of the vocabulary and concepts.

To gather evidence of students' understanding of content-specific text, Palincsar and Schleppegrell (2014) found that teachers commonly asked students to respond to a journal prompt. This example supported the following principles that guided the authors' work: (1) discussing the meaning of the language in small groups and whole-class situations, (2) allowing ELs to use the language and bolstering learning of academic language, and (3) understanding grade-level texts and assignments when aided through the process of focusing on meaning in context by a teacher. Overall, the research revealed that these strategies facilitated student comprehension.

Rationale

In the current U.S. school climate of standards-based learning, teachers need to consider the following to best support ELs in attaining academic success: use of language theories, content learning, language development, and second language learning. These strategies should be used in conjunction with various grade-level texts and assignments. Consistent with Palincsar and Schleppegrell's (2014) vision, we (teacher-researchers Tamra and Patricia) focused on developing and honing the use of metalanguage as a comprehension tool.

The Palincsar and Schleppegrell (2014) research cited in this chapter focused on language and sociocultural theory and research for elementary-aged students; however, we saw connections for the learning of standards-based social studies vocabulary and concepts through the use of illustrated books similar to those used in the summer literacy institute. The specific supports—building prior knowledge; consideration of students' experiences and interest; use of graphic organizers, metalanguage, and vocabulary instruction—supported the high school ELs' comprehension and learning.

According to Rosenblatt's (1978) transactional theory of aesthetic reading, the literature used can create or "stir up" an emotional connection for the reader. Based on this theory and the experiences using illustrated books the previous summer when working with the high school students, the teachers selected *One Thousand Tracings: Healing the Wounds of WWII* by Lita Judge (2007) as the aesthetic reading text. We chose this text because its true life events place the reader into the characters' struggle to aid others' survival immediately following WWII.

Along with these supports, we utilized translanguaging, or using a person's full linguistic repertoire (García & Kleyn, 2016). In a translanguaging classroom, the teacher believes the students have one linguistic repertoire and addresses the four purposes for translanguaging:

1. supporting comprehension of complex text

2. encouraging discussion around academic text

3. creating a space for bilingualism

4. nurturing students' socioemotional needs and bilingual identities

By taking on a translanguaging stance, teachers ensure that the instruction and assessment employed are socially just by leveraging students' bilingualism and full linguistic repertoires (García, Johnson, & Seltzer, 2017).

In light of this theory, we developed a lesson that provided opportunities for the students to use all their language skills when completing the classroom assignments. Throughout the lesson, we built in opportunities for students to use their first and second languages. For example, we provided informational text in Spanish and English, clarified unknown words, utilized small-group conversations, and had students complete and present their ideas from the graphic organizer.

The Palincsar and Schleppegrell (2014) theories were originally used in an elementary science context, but we felt the notions could be easily applied in a high school social studies setting. When used in combination with translanguaging, students would be equipped with powerful strategies in which to comprehend grade-level content-specific vocabulary, concepts, and texts. Through use of these notions, we expect that greater attainment of the grade-level academic standards will occur.

Lesson Plan

Lesson Plan Title	Healing the Wounds of WWII
Grade/Subject Area	Grades 10–11; Integrated social studies and English language arts
Duration	2 (90-minute) class periods
Proficiency Levels	Texas English Language Proficiency Standards (Texas Education Agency, 2009): Beginner to Advanced

(continued on next page)

Lesson Plan *(continued)*	
Content and Language Objectives	Students will be able to • identify a cause/effect relationship of WWII. (Content) • demonstrate understanding of new concepts through a journal reflection. (Content) • use my background knowledge to write and explain what I know about WWII. (Language) • use context clues and resources in English and Spanish (Google Translate, peers, dictionaries, pictures) to define unknown words. (Language) • articulate the reasons for a cause/effect relationship. (Language) • make a self-to-text connection. (Language)
Alignment to Standards	**Common Core State Standards** (NGA & CCSSO, 2018) • *CCSS.ELA-LITERACY.RH.9-10.4*: Determine the meaning of words and phrases as they are used in a text, including vocabulary describing political, social, or economic aspects of history/social science. • *CCSS.ELA-LITERACY.L.9-10.3*: Apply knowledge of language to understand how language functions in different contexts, to make effective choices for meaning or style, and to comprehend more fully when reading or listening. • *CCSS.ELA-LITERACY.RH.11-12.7*: Integrate and evaluate multiple sources of information presented in diverse formats and media (e.g., visually, quantitatively, as well as in words) in order to address a question or solve a problem. • *CCSS.ELA-LITERACY.L.11-12.3*: Apply knowledge of language to understand how language functions in different contexts, to make effective choices for meaning or style, and to comprehend more fully when reading or listening. **Texas Essential Knowledge & Skills: Social Studies** (Texas Education Code) • *§113.41(c)(7)(D)*: Analyze major issues of World War II, including the Holocaust; the internment of German, Italian, and Japanese Americans and Executive Order 9066; and the development of conventional and atomic weapons. • *§113.41(c)(29)*: The student applies critical-thinking skills to organize and use information acquired from a variety of valid sources, including electronic technology. The student is expected to: — *(B)*: Analyze information by sequencing, categorizing, identifying cause-and-effect relationships, comparing and contrasting, finding the main idea, summarizing, making generalizations, making predictions, drawing inferences, and drawing conclusions.

(continued on next page)

Picture This! Using Illustrated Books to Support Comprehension

83

Lesson Plan *(continued)*	
Alignment to Standards *(continued)*	**Texas English Language Proficiency Standards** (Texas Education Code) • *§74.4(c)(1)*: Cross-curricular second language acquisition/learning strategies. The ELL uses language learning strategies to develop an awareness of his or her own learning processes in all content areas. In order for the ELL to meet grade-level learning expectations across the foundation and enrichment curriculum, all instruction delivered in English must be linguistically accommodated (communicated, sequenced, and scaffolded) commensurate with the student's level of English language proficiency. The student is expected to: — *(A)*: use prior knowledge and experiences to understand meanings in English. — *(C)*: use strategic learning techniques such as concept mapping, drawing, memorizing, comparing, contrasting, and reviewing to acquire basic and grade-level vocabulary. — *(D)*: speak using learning strategies such as requesting assistance, employing non-verbal cues, and using synonyms and circumlocution (conveying ideas by defining or describing when exact English words are not known). — *(E)*: internalize new basic and academic language by using and reusing it in meaningful ways in speaking and writing activities that build concept and language attainment.
Outcomes	Students will • generate a list of prior knowledge about WWII. • clarify unknown words in English and Spanish. • produce a written reflection in the form of a journal entry. • complete a graphic organizer in English and Spanish. • discuss the cause/effect relationships of WWII in English and Spanish.
Materials	• Post-it notes • Chart paper • "What Was the Holocaust?" article (Introduction to the Holocaust, n.d.) in Spanish and English • Highlighters • World map • *One Thousand Tracings: Healing the Wounds of WWII* (Judge, 2007) • Computers or devices with internet access • Markers • Colored pencils • Writing journals • Various books about the effects of WWII (see Additional Resources)

Highlighted Teaching Strategies

In this lesson, strategies include brainstorming and translanguaging, incorporation of metalanguage, and allowing student choice in selecting texts. To preassess student background knowledge, you will ask the students to brainstorm what they know about WWII by writing their ideas on Post-it notes. Clarify what it means to brainstorm, because commonly used sayings may have both a literal and figurative meaning. Ensure the students understand the directions so you're able to appropriately assess background knowledge. As the students are writing, encourage them to write down their thoughts in either of their languages. Talking to others in both first and second languages will further help stimulate their thinking during the brainstorm activity.

For translanguaging, you will give the students a copy of the article "Introduction to the Holocaust" (n.d.) in Spanish and English. However, the students are given the option to read in the language that will best support their learning. While reading, you will encourage them to talk to each other in either language they choose. All writing is permitted, and even encouraged, in both languages. Students highlight unknown words and then use context clues, looking at the surrounding text, to understand their meaning. If a student needs more support, they or you can use Google Translate. This translanguaging strategy contributes to equitable learning by providing text in students' first language rather than requiring students to read in English.

The strategy of metalanguage, talking about language, is used to assist the students' comprehension of the informational text. You will use a graphic organizer to teach text structure and to draw attention to the similarities and differences between the English and Spanish text. Regardless of the language in a text, basic structures apply to informational text, such as timeline or cause-and-effect structures. When

Figure 1. Brainstorming graphic organizer.

completing the graphic organizer, the metalanguage strategy prompts conversation about the organization of how the text is presented.

In Spanish, the words *El Holocausto*, *perseguido*, and *mal trato*, and in English, *the Holocaust*, *persecuted*, and *maltreatment* are easily translated. Cognates are useful in some cases, but not in others. Other content words, such as *murdered*, *starvation*, and *envelope*, lack similarity to their Spanish counterparts *asesinado, inanición*, and *sobre,* and may require the use of Google Translate to help the students make meaning. Students will also interact with you in small-group discussions, breaking down other words with similar features. This strategy provides students a space to converse about language in a way that helps them understand the lesson.

Engaging the students' interests and motivation to read is accomplished through the use of a variety of texts: an article, an author's website, and an illustrated book. The students are able to make connections when you read the illustrated book aloud and promote student-generated discussions. After reading the illustrated book, you will have the students explore the author's website (www.tracings.litajudge.com; or link directly from the companion website for this book) by using an iPad (or other device), which includes secondary WWII sources, such as archived pictures of the actual letters, drawings, and characters from the story.

Procedures
Class 1
Begin by introducing students to the lesson by asking, "What do you know about WWII?" Students should brainstorm what they know and ask questions. They might ask questions like, "Was Poland in the war?" Use flexibility in the lesson plan to allow student-generated inquiry and to facilitate discussion. Post-it notes are then used to annotate thoughts and ideas. Then, give students instructions to read an informational text titled, "What Was the Holocaust?" to help build background knowledge. Provide this text in both Spanish and English; however, ask students to read in Spanish first and highlight any unfamiliar vocabulary. Have students work in small groups or pairs to read the text.

After reading and identifying vocabulary, give students time to ask questions about unknown words. Work with small groups to support the students in breaking down difficult vocabulary by using animated gestures, parsing words, and utilizing peer-to-peer support and also Google Translate. The students should identify examples of words that look familiar, such as the English term *Holocaust* and Spanish term *Holocausto*. Other examples of content vocabulary the students may ask about include *starvation, persecuted, incarceration, maltreatment,* and *deplorable.*

Next, introduce the autobiographical book, *One Thousand Tracings: Healing the Wounds of WWII,* written and illustrated by Lita Judge (2007). The book is written as a timeline with short journal-style excerpts from the author's life. The main character is based on the author's grandmother and her past experiences. We chose this story because it takes place after the war and illustrates real events. The paper tracings depicted in the book are from thousands of feet belonging to strangers from Europe who had been left destitute from the war. For example, the June 1947 entry reads, "Soon a thousand tracings lined the walls and floors. A thousand tracings waiting

Figure 2. Brainstorming with Post-it notes.

for shoes like rows of trees waiting for rain." The tracings compelled the author's grandmother and the community to aid these families with the basic necessities for survival.

Students sit in a semicircle as you read the book aloud in English and give language support to students by pointing to pictures, clarifying vocabulary, and making text-to-self connections. The illustrations help the students comprehend the text. According to Stewart (2017), books presented in illustrative formats engage older learners and make text easier to comprehend. One way you can highlight the term *hand-me-down*, found in the text, is by encouraging students to connect their own experiences with clothes given to them by an older relative. During reading, encourage students to ask questions and make comments. An example from the first day of the lesson in Tamra and Patricia's class is excerpted here. At this point in the lesson, the sentence "They're starving" was read, and a new immigrant student from Venezuela named Reyna raised her hand.[2]

Reyna: Miss, we read the word, *starving* from the other reading [referring to the informational text].

Patricia: What is the Spanish word for *starving?*

---

[2] All student names are pseudonyms.

Picture This! Using Illustrated Books to Support Comprehension

87

Reyna:	*inanicion*
Tamra:	You made a text-to-text connection. You recognized a vocabulary word we had discussed earlier from the Holocaust article. [Several of the students had highlighted the word *starvation* as an unknown word because the word in Spanish is dissimilar to the English word].
Reyna:	In Venezuela, there are people who are starving because they have no way to get to a store because of danger of being shot.
Patricia:	Tell us more about your experience.
Reyna:	When I came to America I went to Walmart and there was everything I needed in one store like medicine, food, and clothes. I was surprised. In Venezuela, food is in one place and medicine in another place.
Tamra:	How do people get food?
Reyna:	When it is safe you can go to a store but when you do go to the store the food is expensive. But it is dangerous to leave your house if there are soldiers in the street. [Other students from Venezuela nodded heads in agreement and exchanged words with Reyna in Spanish and English].
Patricia:	So starving can have different meanings for different people depending on your circumstances. The people in our book were being persecuted by the lack of food. Unless a person was high-ranking, a person would not have access to food. You would get nothing.

After the read-aloud, bring out a set of devices and model how to manipulate the features on the author's website (www.tracings.litajudge.com). Research supports the importance of including new literacy instruction into lessons to afford students critical reading opportunities beyond print-based text needed for the 21st century (Alvermann, 2008). The author's website features authentic artifacts, like letters, pictures, and a timeline, and it provides students with a virtual space to explore, manipulate, and access information in a way that would not be possible with paper-based text. It also creates an opportunity to further the students' understanding by answering their questions, affirming their thoughts and ideas, and connecting the story to their own lived experiences. Spend individual time with students to help them access links from the author's site to view items such as foot tracings (based on the title of the book), letters and postcards, and articles of clothing depicted in the illustrated book. Combined with the aesthetic features of the illustrated book and previously read informational text, the variety of texts will help extend the students' understanding of World War II. The day closes with your asking the students to write a reflection on the lesson. Use these student reflections to check for understanding.

Class 2

Start the day reviewing what was covered in the previous session by assessing what the students have learned. Ask them to explain to another student what they learned about the effects of WWII. This also gives the students an opportunity to activate their background knowledge from the previous lesson. Next, remind the students that the reason you chose the topic of WWII is because it was not just part of U.S. history but also world history; share that the purpose and plan for this day's lesson and activity is related to cause and effect relationships for WWII. Give students a copy of *One Thousand Tracings: Healing the Wounds of WWII*, their vocabulary, their copies of the article ("What Was the Holocaust"), and an iPad to revisit the author website.

Ask the students if they're familiar with the terms *cause* and *effect*. If they're not, give an example, such as, "When I came in today, did you notice that I was sweaty and my face was red? What would be the cause?" Allow discussion on cause and effect to continue and have students provide their own examples.

Introduce the students to a graphic organizer to record causes and effects of WWII in English and Spanish. As a scaffolding strategy, provide the cause. Let students know they can use the article, the book, the website, and each other to help them to identify the effects. After completing the concept map, have each student share in English what they wrote and why. In closing the lesson, ask the students to reflect in their journals on the day's lesson and their understanding of the causes and effects of the war. Give students time in class to write (see Figure 3).

Extensions

Extension ideas for this lesson are various. With more time, extension activities could include allowing students to act out what they read, such as in a readers' theater format with the original script written by students or use of an already created script.

Figure 3. Students writing in class.

Students could also hold a debate choosing a topic from the effects of WWII, or create book commercials featuring the elements of problem/solution or cause/effect for the various picture books used. Additionally, they could do activities focusing on comparison and contrast, such as a compare and contrast essay or discussion on various authors' stories on effects of WWII. They could further compare and contrast the language used in primary and secondary sources as related to WWII.

To learn more about WWII and the Holocaust, students could have a virtual (or real) field trip to a Holocaust or WWII museum (for potential online museums, see the online resources on the companion website for this book). Following such activities, students could collaboratively create a "read, write, think: critical thinking map" to guide student-led discussions on social issues, both past and present; write autobiographies in which they record an event, person, object, or feeling associated with every letter of the alphabet; or write personal autobiographies using a Bio Cube. A Bio Cube is a cube that has individualized prompts that ask for descriptions of significant points or people in a student's life and give background information and insight into their personality.

Caveats

The social studies lesson described here was implemented in an after-school small group but could easily be carried out in a whole-class format. Also, although the lesson was not taught in conjunction with a larger unit of study, it met the state and Common Core standards. The two parts of the lesson were delivered a week apart because we only had access to the students once a week. For more continuity, it would be ideal to conduct the lesson in a contiguous format.

Further, though specific illustrated books were used in this lesson with high school ELs, you must consider any unknown lived experiences of your particular students. That is, it is important to consider a student's background and history when selecting books for sensitive lessons. Use of illustrated books can be beneficial in that such books can allow the opportunity for the students to easily make text-to-self connections, which in turn can help you to better know your students. However, you must also understand that it is necessary to consider the students' possible lived experiences in their countries of origin. In our group, having previously worked with the students, we were aware of some similarities between the struggles of the ELs in the book club and the people during WWII (such as war, murder, starvation, and maltreatment) and tried to accommodate for any feelings of trauma.

Assessment and Evaluation

Use the brainstorming activity during the first lesson as a preassessment to determine the student's' prior knowledge of WWII. This is important, especially if your students have some social studies instruction in a country other than the United States. You can preassess students' prior knowledge using their Post-it notes in addition to the conversation among them. This activity reveals the students' wide range of knowledge, from knowing WWII was a war to participating countries.

Use the highlighted article on the Holocaust to gain insight into the strategies students use to learn the meaning of a word. Students may be able to easily read and comprehend words with similar spellings in Spanish and English. Students might be unfamiliar with words like *inanción* [starvation] and *eutanasia* [euthanasia] and highlight them. This gives students the opportunity to learn a vocabulary term first in Spanish and then in English. Use the final reflection to assess what the students have learned from the 2-day lesson. In Tamra and Patricia's group, student journal entries showed themes of family, helping others, and overcoming hardships (see Figure 4).

The journal reflection at the close of each lesson serves as the formative assessment for the day's learning outcomes. The recounting of the first lesson by the students is a formative check to determine what the students remember from the first lesson. The graphic organizer for cause/effect can also be used as a formative assessment.

A postlesson written reflection, in English and/or Spanish, can be used as summative assessment. Reflection allows the students time to solidify their learning.

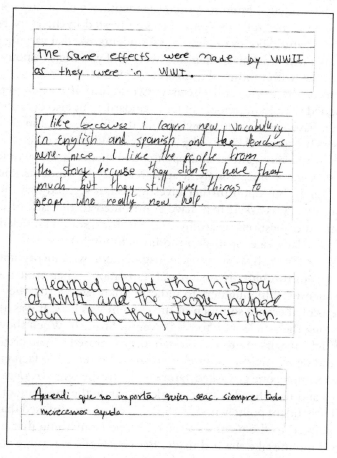

Figure 4. Students' journal entries.

Picture This! Using Illustrated Books to Support Comprehension

91

Reflection on and Analysis of the Lesson

Overall, the lesson was a success. Using an informational text as well as a picture book turned out to be a good decision. At first, we were not sure about use of the picture book, *A Thousand Tracings: Healing the Wounds of World War II*, as it could have been construed as babyish by the high schoolers; however, the decision to include the book in the lesson was based on positive feedback provided by the students in the book club in the previous summer. All of the books used in the book club had been carefully chosen to show diverse characters depicted as protagonists. The book in this lesson was no different.

There was a highly noticeable shift in the students' demeanor from reading the informational text to listening to the children's book. The physical arrangement of the students changed from sitting in desks to sitting in a semicircle where the students' facial expressions were evident. This configuration worked well for the reading and revealed students' interest and engagement, as well as any confusion they were experiencing. The students seemed more invested in the story because of its autobiographical nature. For example, several students asked at varying points in the book if this was a true story and when they were told yes, their response was enthusiastic and effusive, with multiple expressions of "Wow!"

The theme of the causes and effects of World War II was chosen as a lesson because it aligned with high school content standards, but also because we believed our ELs would have some prior knowledge of this from school in their country of origin. To assess background knowledge, we asked, "What do you know about World War II?" This was a very general and open-ended question that would allow for a wide range of answers. Surprisingly, it appeared that the students knew very little about World War II, but upon further investigation, it seemed that the language in which the question was asked may have contributed to the lack of clarity. Going forward, posing the questions regarding students' background knowledge should be done in the home language, Spanish, in addition to English.

When use of Spanish as a translanguaging tool was incorporated, students appeared to benefit through discussion and translation. When students read first in Spanish and then used highlighters to indicate unknown words, they seemed very stressed, ostensibly because so much of the content was new. It was also surprising to note how long the article took to read, even in Spanish. When they were able to discuss the article in pairs or groups, though, they appeared to gain clarity they didn't have when reading on their own. Use of Spanish also served to facilitate vocabulary learning. For example, one girl asked Tamra to define the word *envelope*. Tamra heard her say *envelop* and used hand gestures to demonstrate the meaning of *envelop* as "to surround." The student politely nodded but looked more confused than ever! When the student pointed to the picture of the envelope (something that holds a letter), Tamra realized the mistake she had made. Because Holly was there and was able to translate the word into Spanish and the meaning, it was clear that use of the student's first language greatly helped in constructing meaning from the vocabulary.

Finally, the connections the students made to their own lives from the book were rich, authentic, and valuable and provided opportunity for students to produce rich language. Rosenblatt's (1978) theory of aesthetic reading held true when the students read and discussed the theme of WWII in the informational book and the picture book. Unlike students we had taught previously, these students seemed to have an insider perspective; they could identify with the themes of persecution: hunger, fear, and prejudice. We realized the importance in knowing their struggles coming to a new country and having to learn an entirely new language. This was a reminder of the importance of knowing ELs' experiences and affirming their stories—far more valuable than a lesson or a state standard. The heart of any lesson begins with caring and embracing the newcomers who come into our classrooms. Learning begins with the relationship.

In the final reflections, though none of the students used the academic language of "cause and effect," their reflections confirmed their understanding that WWII did, in fact, have effects on people. Interestingly, the effects were represented in a positive light, such as "people helped when they weren't rich" and "although their family in a bad situation and they receive help they also think in other people and families that also need that thing." The illustrated book served as an authentic text that was relevant and meaningful to students. Future lessons addressing political and geographic information required by social studies standards and objectives could build on their connections.

The students' journals revealed some insightful comments regarding their reflection on the readings and the lesson overall. In some cases, students shared their connections to past knowledge, as in the following excerpt:

- "The same effects were made by WWII as they were in WWI."

Other students reflected on what they learned with regard to new content learning:

- "I learned about the history of WWII and the people helped even when they weren't rich."

- "I like because I learn new vocabulary in English and spanish and the teachers were nice. I like the people from the story because they didn't have that much but they still give things to people who really need help.'

- "I know how people were kill in the WWII and how family were sad because the dead separated there family."

- "Today was a great day because am learn more about the family's that are separated and differents countries. I liked this class."

And the majority of the students' journals reflected on emotional interactions with the texts and lessons[3]:

- "Sometimes is hard to believe that all those stories really happen, but when you see how the world it is today is when you realize that those stories are true."

- "*Aprendi que no importa que seas siempre todos merecinos ayuda.* [I learned that it doesn't matter who you are, everyone deserves help always]"

---

[3] Student writing is quoted verbatim to retain authenticity.

Picture This! Using Illustrated Books to Support Comprehension

93

- "Of the story what I like was that although that family was in a bad situation and they receive help they also think in other people and families that also need that things."

Lastly, though we wanted to use translanguaging as a strategy with the ELs, but didn't speak Spanish, there was some confusion teaching the abstract concepts present in the cause and effect lesson. Another deterrent of not knowing Spanish was that the students were able to talk in Spanish and we didn't have any way of knowing if they were actually talking about the lesson.

Overall, though, one of the largest takeaways of teaching this lesson with the ELs was the power of human connection when teaching history. Our students were able to make personal connections to the people during this period in world history because of their lived experiences in their countries of origin. The illustrated book was a perfect segue into teaching required standards because of the interest and engagement the students showed during the activities.

Additional resources for this chapter are available at www.tesol.org/practices-highschool.

Tamra Dollar is a doctoral student in reading education at Texas Woman's University, Denton, Texas, USA.

Patricia Flint is a doctoral student in special education at Texas Woman's University, Denton, Texas, USA.

Holly Hansen-Thomas is professor of bilingual/ESL at Texas Woman's University, Denton, Texas, USA and is the principal investigator and co-principal investigator of two U.S. Department of Education professional development grants.

References

Alvermann, D. E. (2008). Why bother theorizing adolescents' online literacies for classroom practice and research? *Journal of Adolescent & Adult Literacy, 52*(1), 8–19.

García, O., Johnson, S. I., & Seltzer, K. (2017). *The translanguaging classroom: Leveraging student bilingualism for learning.* Philadelphia, PA: Caslon.

García, O., & Kleyn, T. (2016). *Translanguaging with multilingual students: Learning from classroom moments.* New York, NY: Routledge.

Halliday, M. A. K. (1978). *Language as social semiotic.* London, England: Edward Arnold.

Introduction to the Holocaust. (n. d.). Retrieved from https://www.ushmm.org/wlc/es/article.php?ModuleId=10005751

Judge, L. (2007–2008). *One thousand tracings: Healing the wounds of World War II.* Retrieved from http://www.tracings.litajudge.com/

Judge, L. (2007). *One thousand tracings: Healing the wounds of World War II.* New York, NY: Hyperion Books for Children.

National Governors Association Center for Best Practices (NGA), & Council of Chief State School Officers (CCSSO). (2018). English language arts standards. Washington, DC: Author. Retrieved from http://www.corestandards.org/ELA-Literacy/

Palincsar, A. S., & Schleppegrell, M. J. (2014). Focusing on language and meaning while learning with text. *TESOL Quarterly, 48,* 616–623. doi:10.1002/tesq.178

Rosenblatt, L. M. (1978). *The reader, the text, the poem: Transactional theory of the literary work.* Carbondale, IL: Southern Illinois University Press.

Stewart, M. A. (2017). *Keep it R.E.A.L.! Relevant, engaging and affirming literacy for adolescent English learners.* New York, NY: Teachers College Press & National Writing Project.

Texas Education Agency. (2018). Texas essential knowledge and skills (TEKS). Retrieved from https://tea.texas.gov/index2.aspx?id=6148

Texas Education Agency. (2009). English language proficiency standards (ELPS). Austin, TX: Author. Retrieved from http://www.esc4.net/Assets/telpas-plds.pdf

Texas Education Code §113. Texas Essential Knowledge and Skills for Social Studies. Subchapter C. High School.

Vygotsky, L. (1986). *Thought and language.* Cambridge, MA: MIT Press.

Additional Resources

Teacher resources for using illustrated books with adolescent ELs

Bunting, E., & Himler, R. (1992). *The Wall.* New York, NY: Houghton Mifflin.
Topics Covered: Post-Vietnam War, veterans' memorial, patriotism
Additional Information: Narrative (historical fiction); this picture book helps students think critically about the effects of war and its impact on veterans and their families.

Introduction to the Holocaust. (n. d.). Retrieved from https://www.ushmm.org/wlc/es/article.php?ModuleId=10005751

Lee-Tai, A. (2006). *A place where sunflowers grow.* New York, NY: Children's Book Press.
Topics Covered: World War II, hope, self-expression, Japanese-American internment camps
Additional Information: Narrative (historical fiction); this picture book portrays how a young girl found hope and self-expression through art after being forced into an internment camp. Text is written in English and Japanese.

Lee, M. (1997). *Nim and the war effort.* New York, NY: Farrar, Straus and Giroux.
Topics Covered: Paper shortage during WWII, family heritage
Additional Information: Narrative (historical fiction); based on the author's memories, this picture book explores the challenge of embracing a new culture while maintaining cultural traditions.

Mochizuki, K., & Lee, D. (1997). *Passage to freedom: The Sugihara story.* New York: NY: Lee & Low Books.
Topics Covered: Holocaust, persecution, survival
Additional Information: Narrative (biography); this true life account depicts how a Japanese diplomat used his powers to go against his government to save thousands of Jews.

Moss, M. (2013). *Barbed wire baseball.* New York, NY: Abrams Books for Young Readers.
Topics Covered: Pearl Harbor, perseverance, baseball, Japanese-American internment camps
Additional Information: Narrative (biography); this true story shows how a successful Japanese American baseball player, Kenichi Zenimura (Zeni), brought hope into the internment camp when he started a baseball team.

Rubin, S. G. (2011). *Irena Sendler and the children of the Warsaw Ghetto*. New York, NY: Holiday House.

    Topics Covered: World War II, courage, survival, children of the Holocaust

    Additional Information: Illustrated (biography); Irena Sendler, a Polish social worker, helped nearly 400 Jewish children out of the Warsaw Ghetto and into hiding during World War II.

Ruelle, K. G., & DeSaix, D. D. (2009). *The grand mosque of Paris: A story of how Muslims rescued Jews during the Holocaust*. New York, NY: Holiday House.

    Topics Covered: World War II, humanity, courage, survival, Holocaust

    Additional Information: Illustrated (nonfiction); this true story highlights the kindness of strangers as Muslims hid escaped prisoners of war (Jews, especially children) inside their places of worship.

6

From Research to Practice: Equipping English Learners With History Literacy Skills

Laura Schall-Leckrone, Debbie Barron

Introduction

Because language plays a central role in learning, teachers must develop pedagogical language knowledge to meet the needs of the increasing linguistically diverse student population in U.S. and international contexts (Bunch, 2013; Derewianka & Jones, 2016). This is especially true in secondary history classrooms where concepts are couched in abstract language and complex syntax (Schleppegrell, Greer, & Taylor, 2008). Nonetheless, few history teachers receive sufficient support to incorporate language instruction into content learning for nonnative and nonstandard English speakers. Accordingly, the purpose of this chapter is to describe how a teacher educator and teacher together developed and taught lessons aimed at equipping all students in an urban public high school in the northeastern United States with history literacy skills. The lessons derived from a genre-based framework for integrating history language, content, and thinking skills described by Schall-Leckrone (2017) in an article that built on prior work on genre pedagogy (Derewianka, 1990; Derewianka & Jones, 2016; Gibbons, 2009, 2015) and the language of history (Coffin, 1997, 2006). This chapter presents how genre pedagogy can be used to teach language knowledge in secondary history classrooms. Therefore, the chapter may be of particular interest to English language teachers, history teachers, and history teacher educators as well as a broad group of teachers, teacher educators, applied linguists, and researchers who seek to improve disciplinary literacy instruction for English learners (ELs).

Synopsis of Original Research

Schall-Leckrone, L. (2017). Genre pedagogy: A framework to prepare history teachers to teach language. *TESOL Quarterly, 51*, 358–382. doi:10.1002/tesq.322

The *TESOL Quarterly (TQ)* article, "Genre Pedagogy: A Framework to Prepare History Teachers to Teach Language" (Schall-Leckrone, 2017) recommends that teachers adopt a genre-based framework to promote students' language and conceptual development. Accordingly, this chapter describes how genre pedagogy was used to teach historical explanations in linguistically diverse ninth-grade world history classrooms. Genre pedagogy is an apprenticeship model designed to teach organizational and linguistic features of school genres through instructional phases in which students, before they write independently, develop content knowledge, deconstruct exemplars, and engage in collaborative writing guided by the teacher (see Derewianka & Jones, 2016). Laura (first author) wrote the anchor article based on her dissertation research, in which Debbie (second author)[1] was a participant, so this chapter demonstrates how findings and insights gleaned from a shared earlier research experience were put into practice.

In the anchor article, Laura describes how she followed two study participants (novice history teachers who had completed graduate coursework to prepare them to teach ELs history) into urban U.S. high schools to observe the extent to which they drew on preservice preparation to teach language associated with history. The article starts by identifying challenges of history for ELs and speakers of nonstandard English variations. It includes a review of prior research on teaching history to bilingual learners and descriptions of linguistic components of reading, writing, and conversing in history and how to address them. Then, Laura introduces a specialized form of genre pedagogy and the theory of language at its core, systemic functional linguistics (SFL). SFL is a sociocultural theory of language based on the premise that context, relationships, mode of interaction, and content shape language choices. Laura further explains how SFL has been used to delineate organizational and linguistic features of three key history genres: stories, explanations, and arguments. In brief, stories recount what happened, explanations illuminate causes and consequences of events, and historical arguments promote an interpretation of the past based on evidence.

The next section of the article describes an empirical study in which Laura analyzed the extent to which novice history teachers taught language. Data sources included video-recorded lessons, lesson plans, teaching materials (e.g., handouts and readings), and semistructured interviews. She found the two novice history teachers exhibited promising practices that integrated language and content instruction. For instance, they explicitly taught vocabulary, including both key history concepts

---

[1] In the original article, Debbie was assigned the pseudonym "Sarah" to protect her anonymity.

and general academic terms and phrases; implemented structured group interactions with classmates and authentic historical sources; and taught general literacy strategies, such as how to annotate readings and take notes. However, they did not proactively identify and embed into history lessons linguistic expectations of history tasks and texts (Santos, Darling-Hammond, & Cheuk, 2012). These novice teachers, who had completed targeted preservice preparation and demonstrated promising practices, needed further support to develop and implement pedagogical language knowledge.

Therefore, in the anchor article, Laura proposed a genre-based framework for teaching the language of history that drew from prior work on genre pedagogy (Derewianka, 1990; Derewianka & Jones, 2016; Gibbons, 2009, 2015), history genres (Coffin, 1997, 2006), and her classroom research. The framework outlines the purpose, organizational, and linguistic features of the following history genres: stories, explanations, and arguments. For instance, story genres retell events in the past, so students might use a timeline to chronicle historic events with time references, named individuals, and past tense action verbs. Historical explanations address the causes and consequences of phenomena in the past, so they often incorporate dense noun groups/nominalizations and cause-effect verbs such as *determined* or *led to*. Historical arguments promote an interpretation of the past based on evidence. This genre uses present tense, no-human abstract participants, and rhetorical devices, such as thesis statements and evaluative language.

In the anchor article, Laura illustrates how to teach these history genres with classroom vignettes from secondary history classrooms, including activities with a linguistic focus, excerpts from texts, and graphic organizers. In the process, she argues explicit language instruction can be paired with the use of graphic organizers as part of genre pedagogy to support ELs' language and literacy development in content classes (Harper & de Jong, 2004).

In the remainder of this chapter, we demonstrate why and how we used the research framework from the anchor article as the impetus to develop and implement an instructional unit based on genre pedagogy to teach ELs and their monolingual classmates to write historical explanations. Then, we present one of the lessons from that unit, on identifying examples of cause-effect language in a historical explanation.

Rationale

We had compatible reasons for choosing to use the *TESOL Quarterly* article (Schall-Leckrone, 2017) as the starting point for collaborative work aimed at equipping linguistically diverse adolescents to write historical explanations, primary among them that we had been engaged as practitioner (Laura) and participant (Debbie), in the original study. Laura sought an opportunity to implement the framework described in the anchor article and study the results. Further, she believed that teacher and teacher educator learning related to meeting the needs of ELs in content classrooms (or any topic for that matter) is an ongoing, developmental process. Graduate coursework is a good start, but insufficient in fully preparing even accomplished aspiring teachers to teach the language demands of their content area (Garrone-Shufran,

2015; Schall-Leckrone, 2017). Based on the findings of her earlier research, she believed collaboration and site-based coaching would be a more supportive approach to equipping novice history teachers to teach history language, content, and thinking skills (also see Nagle, 2014).

As a research participant, Debbie became interested not only in the content of the original study (Schall-Leckrone, 2017), but also in the research process itself, so Laura invited Debbie to engage in a collaborative study after her dissertation was complete. Debbie believed that her students would benefit from more focused attention to writing in a history classroom. Together, we decided to develop and implement an instructional unit for Debbie's ninth-grade world history classes focused on using genre pedagogy to teach historical explanations, based on the developmental needs of Debbie's students. As early adolescents, most of her students had practiced writing stories in the form of personal narratives throughout their primary school years. They would be expected to develop the analytical skills and linguistic resources to write arguments based on evidence as they advanced through secondary school and into higher education. Learning to craft historical explanations could play a pivotal role in Debbie's students' development as writers, because explanations require that students understand the logic of interrelated causes and consequences and use the language of causation and evaluation to explain factors triggering and resulting from significant phenomena (see Coffin, 2006).

Overall, we were interested in putting this research into practice because we shared a commitment to improving learning opportunities for ELs in history classes as a matter of social justice. That is, we believed that ELs should receive equitable access to rigorous authentic content and have the opportunity to develop disciplinary and critical literacy skills associated with academic achievement. Debbie was teaching world history classes in a comprehensive high school in a small city within a large metropolitan area in the northeastern United States.

The city recently had experienced a dramatic increase in its population of immigrants and children of immigrants. Approximately 30% of students in Debbie's honors classes spoke a home language other than English; this percentage was even higher in classes designated as "standard" classes, with 41% of students speaking another home language. The academic vocabulary, morphological forms, and syntax of history, particularly in authentic historical sources, were unfamiliar to the vast majority of students, including monolingual English speakers. Through the development of lessons derived from the framework for teaching history genres described in the anchor article, we sought to increase opportunities for all learners, and especially ELs, to improve their analytical, reading, and writing skills in history. We focused on integrating language and literacy skills into regular history instruction through genre pedagogy.

Lesson Plan

Lesson Plan Title	Finding the Language of Cause and Effect in a Historical Explanation
Grade/Subject Area	Grade 9; World history I
Duration	90 minutes
Proficiency Levels	WIDA (2007): Levels 4–6 (Expanding to Reaching)
Content and Language Objectives	Students will be able to • explain at least three reasons early Rome expanded, including economic, military, and political factors. (Content) • identify complex sentences that show cause and effect using verbs such as *led to, caused,* or *brought about* from the exemplar text (reading). (Language) • distinguish causes from effects and identify language structures (verb phrases and connecting words) used to show cause and effect and record them on a graphic organizer (writing). (Language)
Alignment to Standards	**Common Core State Standards** (NGA & CCSSO, 2018) • *CCSS.ELA-LITERACY.RH.9-10.3*: Analyze in detail a series of events described in a text; determine whether earlier events caused later ones or simply preceded them. • *CCSS.ELA-LITERACY.RH.9-10.5*: Analyze how a text uses structure to emphasize key points or advance an explanation or analysis. • *CCSS.ELA-LITERACY.RH.9-10.4*: Determine the meaning of words and phrases as they are used in a text, including vocabulary describing political, social, or economic aspects of history/social science. **Massachusetts History and Social Science Curriculum Framework** (Massachusetts Department of Education, 2003) • *Grades 8–12 Concepts and Skills: History and Geography (5)*: Explain how a cause and effect relationship is different from a sequence or correlation of events. (H, C, E) • *Grade 7 Concepts and Skills: 7.36*: Explain how the geographical location of ancient Rome contributed to the shaping of Roman society and the expansion of its political power in the Mediterranean region and beyond. (H, G, E)
Outcomes	Students will • identify the language used to express cause and effect in historical explanations. • create a list of cause/effect language that will be used throughout the unit.

(continued on next page)

Lesson Plan *(continued)*	
Materials	• Appendixes A and B (available on the companion website for this book) — Exemplar text: Roman Expansion (Appendix A) — Word wall with cause and effect language (Appendix B) • Cause/effect graphic organizer • Projector

Highlighted Teaching Strategies

The genre-based unit consists of lessons intended to apprentice students into the language, content, and thinking skills needed to write historical explanations. Scaffolding inheres in the teaching-learning cycle (TLC) associated with genre pedagogy (Derewianka & Jones, 2016), which is evident in its phases: building background knowledge, modeling and deconstructing the genre, co-construction, and then independent writing. The approach is constructivist, building on what students already know, while introducing new content and language through modeling, structured whole-group then small-group activities, and gradually releasing responsibility to the students to demonstrate individual mastery in written compositions. Here, a lesson is featured from the deconstruction phase of the TLC during which students work in groups to explain the reasons that early Rome expanded by identifying examples of cause and effect logic and language.

Procedures

Before you teach this lesson, preteach the vocabulary term *factor* and acquaint students with the text. For instance, students should use a graphic organizer to outline the text's organization and examine the thesis statement as the roadmap of an essay. The students could also answer comprehension questions and examine the author's purpose. You could explain that, unlike a scientific reaction in which boiling is the direct cause of heating water, historical events do not typically happen in a linear fashion. Often, there are many interrelated factors that precipitate a historical event. Precise and nuanced language is required to write a clear and thoughtful explanation of it. Debbie set the stage for the lesson by explaining to her students:

> We want to be clear when we write this way in history because it's not
> neat. Unlike science when you put water over fire, it's gonna boil.
> That's cause and effect. But, in history when it's the world, and it's
> people and events, it's not neat like that. We can't tie it up in a bow.

Begin the lesson with a warm-up question that prompts students to relate cause and effect logic to everyday life. For instance, they might consider factors that contribute to a student's ability to attend college. After they write freely for several minutes, engage the students in a brief classroom discussion and list student responses on the board. Ultimately, students should realize that no one factor leads to college attendance; rather, interrelated factors make possible significant life events. Then, transition to the idea that the same logic can be applied to history; a culmination of interrelated factors also precipitate historical events.

First, ask students to consider what the prefix *inter–* means in *interact* or *intersect*. A student may respond, "to act together." They should recognize that *inter–* signifies related factors impact one another. In addition, Debbie told her students, "Sometimes nonhuman factors are used to characterize what led to particular events." Then, she read an example from the text, "The spirit of past victories fueled Roman conquests" and noted, "'spirit of victories,' that's not human, right?" Debbie explained that they must learn how to interpret sentences like that, because that is how history is written.

After this introduction, most of the lesson will focus on identifying examples of cause and effect and the language used to express these relationships in the exemplar text, "Roman Expansion" (Appendix A). First, model how to find an example of cause and effect in the exemplar and record this information on a graphic organizer. To do so, project the text on the board and do a read aloud/think aloud. When you read the text out loud and find a complex sentence with an instance of cause and effect, use two different colors of marker to show students how to distinguish the cause from the effect and circle the specific language used. For instance, Debbie discussed this sentence: "This early expansion, in which Rome annexed most of its close neighbors, brought about a period of stability and growth." You can ask your students to help in identifying cause and effect. Then, project the graphic organizer on the board and model how to record the key components of the sentence as demonstrated in Figure 1.

After some guided practice with a couple more examples, direct students to work together (in preselected linguistically heterogeneous groupings) to complete the graphic organizer. Students already should be comfortable working in these groups, and you should have determined in advance that they are functional, thoughtful groupings, as successful engagement in this lesson promotes use of academic talk as demonstrated in the following conversation from Debbie's classroom. Ella, Aimee,

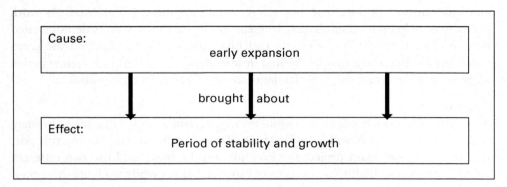

Figure 1. Selection of the cause: effect graphic organizer.

Tim, and Trevor together identified two examples of cause and effect logic from the exemplar and recorded them on their graphic organizers:[2]

Ella:	Where it says [reading], "As in many communities, Rome's economic needs made them engage with their neighbors." And then the [pause], the effect was, "By the year 270 BCE, Rome controlled most of the Italian peninsula."
Trevor:	Whoa, whoa.
Aimee:	Wait, I thought it was, "economic needs" was the cause and then the effect was "they engaged with . . ."
Ella:	Yeah.
Aimee:	". . . their neighbors."
Ella:	No.
Aimee:	Wait [pause], what?
Ella:	No.
Trevor:	The cause was the "economic needs," and then the result was, "they engaged with their neighbors."
Ella:	Okay.
Trevor:	But did you say that?
Ella:	Sure.
Tim:	Now, how 'bout this, "This growth resulted in the immediate need [pause] for even more resources [pause] and populations."
Aimee:	Oh. That's on my other ones.
Ella:	Are we writing this down?

When Ella reads from the text, Aimee points out the cause and effect example in what she read. At first, Ella is unsure, so Trevor ascertains that she understands. Then, Tim points out another example, which Aimee seems to have found as well, and Ella wants to be sure that they are recording the information. Students work together to help each other identify language in the exemplar text, as demonstrated here. Aimee, Tim, and Trevor ensure that Ella understands the task, and she keeps them on task. Because it may be the first time students are analyzing a reading in this manner, it is important that your students are comfortable in their groups.

Closing

To prepare for a teacher-led discussion, prompt certain groups to be ready to share specific examples. This will help direct the class-wide discussion. During this portion of the lesson, again project the exemplar on the board and use two different colors of marker to highlight instances of cause and effect while students share their

---

[2] Student names are pseudonyms; in this group, there are three monolingual students (Ella, Tim, and Trevor) and one bilingual learner (Aimee), who is Haitian.

examples. In addition, keep a running list of the connecting words and verb phrases that express cause and effect on the board, which will be compiled into a word wall of "cause/effect" language that students can reference and use in their own writing (see Appendix B).

Extensions

Toward the lesson's end, lead a brief discussion of how word selection contributes to meaning. You can look at your list of cause and effect language on the board and consider how changing a verb can reveal shades of meaning, as in: "The victory fueled a competitive spirit" instead of "The victory contributed to a competitive spirit." Explain that although the difference is slight, it can be illuminating, much like "eating too much junk food made me vomit" and "eating too much junk food forced me to vomit." The graphic nature of these silly sentences can help students consider how word choices contribute to how we ascribe meaning. To extend the lesson, you could have the students write their own cause and effect sentences, which can be historical or not. They could use the new vocabulary list and explain how different verb choices change the meaning. Similarly, you could spend more time looking at the exemplar and prompt students to rewrite sentences with different verbs or connecting words that serve to strengthen or weaken it. Essentially, you want students to engage with their new language and get comfortable with its use and potential.

Caveats

This lesson follows earlier lessons in the TLC. Thus, for this lesson to succeed, the students must be comfortable with the content and organization of the exemplar text. Additionally, this should not be the first lesson in which these student groups have worked together. You should compose groups that will work together consistently during the unit, carefully considering students' first and second languages, abilities, personalities, unique learning needs/styles, and relationships. They will rely on one another to learn and practice new language both orally and in writing. Finally, the success of the unit for each student is contingent on regular class attendance. Though all teachers build upon what they have previously taught, the TLC depends on the students working through each phase.

Assessment and Evaluation

During this lesson, you will circulate among students during group work to engage in formative assessment. You should assess group dynamics and student comfort with the language. The final class-wide discussion also serves as a formative assessment in which students will identify key examples of cause and effect and you will lead a discussion of the economic, military, and political factors that led to Roman expansion. Finally, the graphic organizers can be collected and evaluated to determine that individual students have met the lesson's content and language objectives.

As the culminating phase of the TLC, students write their own historical explanations, which serve as the summative assessment for the unit. To prepare to write an explanation of the fall of Rome independently, students will continue to work with their groups as they engage in co-construction activities. See Figures 2 and 3 for examples of activities that help students prepare for their final essay.

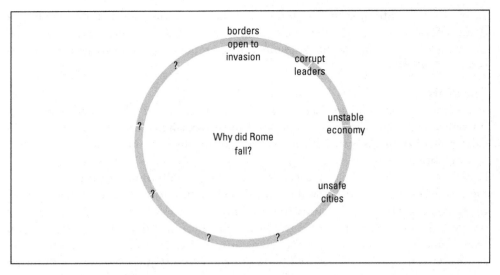

Figure 2. Sample concept web to brainstorm causes of the fall of Rome.

Category 1: Economic factors	Category 2	Category 3::
• Evidence here • More evidence here		

Figure 3. Categorizing factors that led to the fall of Rome.

On this summative assessment, students are evaluated on the content and organization, and their use of the language of cause and effect.

Reflection on and Analysis of the Lesson

We developed and implemented a genre-based instructional unit in ninth-grade world history classes and studied the process. Consistent with the TLC, our approach built on students' prior knowledge as Debbie used everyday examples to help students make sense of new concepts and become proficient in historical language. For instance, she used college admissions to represent how multiple factors precipitate an event and silly sentences about overeating to showcase how verb choices construct nuanced meaning. In addition, through structured group interactions, students built conceptual knowledge and language skills of history as building blocks toward disciplinary literacy. Through the scaffolded interactive steps of genre pedagogy, students appreciated multiple opportunities to develop explicit knowledge about the organization and linguistic features of historical explanations before independently writing one.

Debbie observed significant improvements in student writing after teaching genre-based units (including a second one on the Crusades), especially among ELs. Students' essays had clear structures and thesis statements incorporating causal logic and linguistic features. In fact, most students kept their cause/effect word lists for the remainder of the year and continued to use them unprompted. Overall, our findings were consistent with Laura's proposition in the anchor article (Schall-Leckrone, 2017):

> . . . Focused attention to linguistic features of genres [can] serve as a mechanism to integrate reading, writing, and text-based discussions to promote disciplinary literacy . . . Teaching students how to engage in linguistic analysis with the support of graphic organizers [can] improve comprehension and production of academic texts. (p. 377)

Students engaged all communicative modes to develop oral language, reading, and writing skills of history. That is, they learned how history is constructed through the analytical skills and word choices of historians, who assess and group factors into categories they create to show what precipitated or resulted from significant historical events.

Bunch (2013) stated that it is the teacher's role "to purposefully enact opportunities for the development of language and literacy in and through teaching the core curricular content" (p. 298). Genre pedagogy provides a framework that teachers can use to apprentice ELs in heterogeneous classes into disciplinary literacy skills associated with academic achievement. The lesson presented here is intended to support the work of teachers and teacher educators, who share a commitment to improving learning opportunities for the increasing number of ELs taught in general education classes.

The appendixes for this chapter are available at www.tesol.org/practices-highschool.

Laura Schall-Leckrone, an associate professor and the director of the TESOL and Bilingual Education Programs at the Graduate School of Education at Lesley University, Cambridge, Massachusetts, USA, conducts research in teacher preparation and pedagogies that promote critical literacies for culturally and linguistically diverse students.

Debbie Barron, an experienced high school world history teacher, is adjunct faculty at the Graduate School of Education at Lesley University, Cambridge, Massachusetts, USA, where she teaches a course on how to shelter secondary content instruction and engages in research on teaching writing to culturally and linguistically diverse students.

References

Bunch, G. C. (2013). Pedagogical language knowledge: Preparing mainstream teachers for ELs in the new standards era. *Review of Research in Education, 37*, 298–341.

Coffin, C. (1997). Constructing and giving value to the past: An investigation into secondary school history. In F. Christie & J. R. Martin (Eds.), *Genre and institutions: Social processes in the workplace and school* (pp.196–230). London, England: Cassell.

Coffin, C. (2006). *Historical discourse: The language of time, cause, and evaluation*. London, England: Continuum.

Derewianka, B. (1990). *Exploring how texts work*. Newtown, Australia: Primary English Teaching Association.

Derewianka, B., & Jones, P. (2016). *Teaching language in context* (2nd ed.). South Melbourne, Australia: Oxford University Press.

Garrone-Shufran, S. (2015). *The development of language knowledge in a teacher education program: Preparing secondary teacher education candidates to teach academic English in their content area lessons* (Unpublished doctoral dissertation). Boston College, MA.

Gibbons, P. (2009). *ELs, academic literacy, and thinking: Learning in the challenge zone*. Portsmouth, NH: Heinemann.

Gibbons, P. (2015). *Scaffolding language, scaffolding learning: Teaching English language learners in the mainstream classroom* (2nd ed.). Portsmouth, NH: Heinemann.

Harper, C., & de Jong, E. (2004). Misconceptions about teaching English-language learners. *Journal of Adolescent & Adult Literacy, 48*(2), 152–162.

Massachusetts Department of Education. (2003, August). Massachusetts history and social science curriculum framework. Malden, MA: Author. Retrieved from http://www.doe.mass.edu/frameworks/hss/final.pdf

Nagle, J. (2014). *Creating collaborative learning communities to improve English learner instruction: College faculty, school teachers, and pre-service teachers learning together in the 21st century*. Charlotte, NC: Information Age.

National Governors Association Center for Best Practices (NGA), & Council of Chief State School Officers (CCSSO). (2018). English language arts standards. Washington, DC: Author. Retrieved from http://www.corestandards.org/ELA-Literacy/

Santos, M., Darling-Hammond, L., & Cheuk, T. (2012). Teacher development to support English language learners in the context of the Common Core State Standards. *Understanding language: Language, literacy, and learning in the content areas*. Stanford, CA: Stanford University.

Schall-Leckrone, L. (2017). Genre pedagogy: A framework to prepare history teachers to teach language. *TESOL Quarterly, 51*, 358–382. doi:10.1002/tesq.322

Schleppegrell, M. J., Greer, S., & Taylor, S. (2008). Literacy in history: Language and meaning. *Australian Journal of Language and Literacy, 31*(2), 174–187.

World Class Instructional and Design and Assessment. (2007). English language proficiency standards grade 6 through grade 12. Retrieved from https://www.wida.us/standards/eld.aspx

Section 3

Science

Bilingual Biomes: Revising and Redoing Monolingual Instructional Practices for Multilingual Students

Brian Seilstad, Derek Braun, Somin Kim, Min-Seok Choi

Introduction

This chapter focuses on a specific activity and general pedagogy designed to support multilingual learners' development of English, their home language (L1), and advanced science content. The lesson we share draws on Cummins's (2009) *TESOL Quarterly* article, "Multilingualism in the English-Language Classroom: Pedagogical Considerations," which identifies "common-sense" monolingual instructional strategies as a form of injustice to teachers and learners of English. Cummins (2009) argues for intentional bilingual approaches to support English learners and to "reposition TESOL as a strong advocate for empirically supported and equity-oriented approaches to English language teaching" (p. 320).

The lesson provided in this chapter occurred during a collaborative ethnographic research project with high school teacher Derek Braun, a multilingual speaker of English, Spanish, and Somali who has an MEd in science and endorsement in TESOL. Derek is part of the English as a Second Language (ESL) Program in a Central Ohio, USA, school district that has become a super diverse urban environment characterized by demographic and linguistic shifts in the past 20 years that are highly mobile, complex, and unpredictable (Blommaert, 2013). Today, students in this district collectively speak more than 100 languages with at least five—Spanish, Somali, Nepali, French, and Arabic—major languages represented in many educational contexts. In addition, these students include refugees or other migrants with vastly divergent prior educations, such as high-quality, continuous schooling versus students with limited or interrupted formal education (SLIFE) as well as manifold socioemotional or socioeconomic challenges requiring significant school and community support.

This chapter draws on research with Derek at a 2-year middle/high school newcomer program specifically designed to help this student population, all of whom are identified as either "emerging" or "progressing" according to Ohio's English language proficiency ratings, transition to ESL sheltered site or mainstream schooling. The focal activity in the lesson, the Bilingual Biomes Project, was implemented at the end of the 2015–2016 academic year in Derek's 10th-grade Biology class. Critically, Derek had developed a monolingual version of this biome project the previous year but, as a result of reading the anchor article (Cummins, 2009), changed to the bilingual version, which he continues to improve and use. The 2015–2016 Bilingual Biomes Project was implemented in two different Biology sections, each with 15–20 students from the five aforementioned language groups in addition to others, such as Zomi, Wolof/Fulani, and Swahili. The activity required students to (1) conduct independent research on key ecology topics aligned to district and state standards, (2) prepare a Google Slides document, and (3) present bilingually in their L1 and English.

Synopsis of Original Research

Cummins, J. (2009). Multilingualism in the English-language classroom: Pedagogical considerations. *TESOL Quarterly, 43*, 317–321. doi:10.1002/j.1545-7249.2009.tb00171.x

The Bilingual Biomes Project was supported and expanded by Derek's reflections on the Cummins (2009) article, which challenged the "monolingual principle" common in much TESOL and general language learning pedagogy over the past 100 years. This principle "emphasizes the instructional use of the target language (TL) to the exclusion of the students' home language (L1), with the goal of enabling learners to think in the TL *with minimal interference* [emphasis added] from the L1" (p. 317). The primary issue Cummins (2009) addresses here on both empirical and theoretical grounds is the notion of the L1 as interference rather than a fundamental cognitive and social resource for the language and content learning process. Consolidating a wide body of literature, he challenges these monolingual norms in TESOL by articulating several points arguing for the judicious use of the L1 in instruction to

- build on preexisting knowledge,
- develop translation skills,
- use cognates to build vocabulary,
- encourage L1 biliteracy,
- use bilingual dictionaries, and
- legitimize the L1 as a cognitive tool (pp. 319–320).

These recommendations challenge tensions between methods of English immersion and bilingual education that have existed for some time. However, Cummins (2009) addresses the broader context of equity by pointing out the paradox that, on the one hand, the TESOL community has "consistently articulated its support for bilingual education" (p. 318) but, on the other hand, there exists a reality that many ESL educators, whether because of pedagogical philosophy, personal language skills, or language policy, rarely engage directly with their students' L1. This may contribute to the range of outcomes for adolescent newcomers that may not be satisfactory for many (Suárez-Orozco et al., 2010).

On the other hand, these TESOL patterns are not immutable, and an earlier article by Cummins (2007) illustrates how a group of three seventh-grade Pakistani students in Canada, who were English learners at different levels of proficiency, collaborated to create a bilingual Urdu-English book, referred to as an identity text. This specific text (and identity texts in general) affirmed the students' backgrounds and experiences while increasing the likelihood that language-minority students will receive praise and affirmation in educational settings. Cummins (2007) focuses on one student, Madiha, who speaks "minimal" English but is fluent in Urdu, and points out that "in a 'normal' classroom, Madiha's ability to participate . . . would have been severely limited . . . [but] when the social structure of the classroom was changed . . . [she] was able to express *herself* in ways that few [second language] learners experience" (p. 235). With this changed structure, Cummins (2007) describes how the three students debated orally their book's content in Urdu, drafted an English text together, and then translated that English text into Urdu. The cognitive processes here are also made clear by Madiha herself when she comments, "When I am allowed to use Urdu in class, it helps me because when I write in Urdu and then I look at Urdu words and English comes in my mind" (Cummins, 2007, p. 236). Critically, although Cummins (2007) does not describe the teacher in detail, he provides a glimpse into this teacher's stance by emphasizing that the teacher's lack of Urdu or other home language knowledge did not impede the implementation of bilingual approaches.

Although these Cummins articles (2007, 2009) are relatively recent and just a glimpse of his prolific writing, they address the long-standing dialogue/tension between TESOL as a field and bilingual approaches. In the U.S. context, this is especially salient because language policy holds powerful sway over the learning and teaching contexts available to students, made most evident by the policy shifts in states such as Arizona, California, and Massachusetts. However, research and theory have continued to push on these norms, and Cummins's (2009) article cites the contribution of *translanguaging* (García, Johnson, & Seltzer, 2017), which challenges monolingual understandings of bilingualism (e.g., code-switching) that imagine the speaker alternating between two separate languages rather than deploying a "full linguistic repertoire without regard for watchful adherence to the socially and politically defined boundaries of named (and usually national and state) languages" (Otheguy, García, & Reid, 2015, p. 281). In the classroom, García et al. (2017) point out that bi/multilingualism is a reality that flows through the classroom, a *translanguaging corriente*, that cannot and should not be unnecessarily restricted. At most, this can be silenced, but Cummins (2009) argues that this undermines and delays the participatory possibilities for newcomer students, an effect that can linger for several years and have significant long-term academic and social consequences.

Thus, Cummins (2007, 2009) and García et al. (2017) consistently encourage teachers to consider ways to use the students' L1 for language and content learning. However, intentionality is key, and Cummins (2007) is careful to insist that these reforms not "encourage regression to predominant use of translation nor to dilute the centrality of promoting [second language] communicative interaction in both oral and written modes in [second language] classrooms" (p. 237). In other words, Cummins is not arguing that increasingly complex target language exposure, use, and assessment be forsaken or that L1 development become the primary goal. However, he is pointing out that the L1 and its underlying linguistic development is the foundation for further language learning and that bilingual instructional strategies are important scaffolds and supports to more advanced second language performance. Inspired by Cummins's (2009) article and those related to it, Derek's Bilingual Biomes Project is an attempt to apply and extend these insights in his context of serving super-diverse adolescent newcomer youth.

Rationale

Although most research shows that English language learners would benefit from a bilingual education (Valentino & Reardon, 2015), there remains a general unavailability of bilingual programs throughout the United States (Lewis & Gray, 2016). In employing bilingual instructional strategies in his ESL biology classroom, Derek's pedagogical stance on teaching his ESL students shifted over time in a manner reflective of Cummins's (2009) discussion on the tension between TESOL and bilingual education. In 2015, Derek placed his students in linguistically heterogeneous groups, orienting to the theory that the students would be forced to use English to work together and then present in English. Thus, his first iteration of the project did not create possibilities for the students to use their L1 as a resource. Derek's reflection on this project in the context of his bilingual education course and Cummins's (2009) article inspired the shift to the Bilingual Biomes Project version in which students were put into mainly homogeneous language groups, asked to create a Google Slides presentation in their L1 about a biome from their countries of origin, and tasked with speaking publically in their L1 followed by interpretation to English.

Although the focus of this article is on bilingual approaches and engagement with students' L1 in the multilingual TESOL classroom, the Bilingual Biomes Project is enmeshed in both Derek's and the broader educational ecology today where digital multimodality skills engage students with an array of online and computer-based technologies for learning, research, writing, and presenting. These multimodal practices help students develop multiliteracy skills and critical perspectives on social issues, negotiate their identities, and become motivated to be more autonomous learners (Yi & Angay-Crowder, 2016). Throughout the year, Derek consistently used online multimodal tools, such as Brain Pop (www.brainpop.com) and Flocabulary (www.flocabulary.com) to make the material more accessible, Kahoot! (www.kahoot.com) to motivate the students with online quizzes, and Edmodo (www.edmodo.com) and various Google Drive applications (e.g., Docs, Slides) to communicate with the students and encourage collaboration.

Lesson Plan

Lesson Plan Title	Bilingual Biomes Project
Grade/Subject Area	Grade 10; Biology (English learner sheltered instruction)
Duration	5–7 (90-minute) class periods
Proficiency Levels	Ohio English Language Proficiency Assessment (Ohio Department of Education, 2018): Emerging to Progressing
Content and Language Objectives	Students will be able to • research real-world examples of how producers and consumers interact in an ecosystem. (Content) • use and interpret real-world data to present climate conditions of the focus biome, including monthly average precipitation and temperature. (Content) • describe energy flow within an ecosystem and interactions of organisms within their environment and the flow of energy with in food webs. (Language) • compose informational texts in both English and their first language (L1). (Language) • develop formal language skills in both their L1 and English. (Language) • interpret from their L1 to English. (Language)
Alignment to Standards	**Ohio's New Learning Standards: Science Standards** (Ohio Department of Education, 2011) *Model Curriculum Grade 7: Life Science: Instructional Strategies and Resources:* Research a biome . . . select an organism and find data on the population . . . provide information and data about the biomes of the world (p. 222) **Ohio English Language Proficiency Standards** (Ohio Department of Education, 2015) *ELP 9-12.3:* An English Language Learner can speak and write about grade appropriate complex literary and informational texts and topics. • *Level 5:* By the end of each language proficiency level, an English language learner can — deliver oral presentations. — compose written informational texts. — fully develop the topic with relevant details, concepts, examples, and information. — integrate graphics or multimedia when useful.

(continued on next page)

Lesson Plan *(continued)*	
Outcomes	Students will • develop a deeper understanding of the biology content objectives through the support and use of their L1. • connect their past experiences of living in a certain biome with the content learning objectives. • research and present real-world data and graphs about climate conditions from their chosen biome. • collaborate both in person in the classroom and online through the use of the Google Slides document as they develop content through interpersonal interactions in both their L1 and English. • prepare a Google Slides presentation in a group, giving them multimodal experience with a digital, online form of collaboration. • select a member from the group to present in their L1 first and another student to interpret to English, giving a sense of validation about their L1 as well as developing interpretation skills.

Materials	• Chromebooks or other internet-connected device (classroom set)
	• Projector
	• Bilingual dictionaries
	• Appendixes A and B (available on the companion website for this book)
	   — Bilingual Biomes Project Rubrics (Appendix A)
	   — Bilingual Biomes Project Survey (Appendix B)

Highlighted Teaching Strategies

The strategies employed with the Bilingual Biomes Project are grounded in the principles of content and language integrated learning, perhaps exemplified best in the United States through the Structured Immersion Observation Protocol model (Echevarría, Vogt, & Short, 2012), which seeks to build on students' background knowledge while using the L1 as a resource for learning. In this case, the Bilingual Biomes Project is preceded by several days of direct instruction about biomes during which students learned about biomes from you, collaborative activities and worksheets, and multimedia presentations, such as relevant BrainPOP videos (www. brainpop.com). This instruction is conducted primarily in English, although students are allowed to use their L1 while working independently. In Derek's class, he used Google Translate for key vocabulary terms or spoke to students in Spanish or Somali as necessary to help them understand the material. Thus, these days are designed to provide the students with enough knowledge about the biome topic to engage with the Bilingual Biomes Project.

Then, at the beginning of the Bilingual Biomes Project itself, you present the activity orally using a number of audiovisual tools, check the students' comprehension in various ways, and are prepared to repeat or rephrase as often as necessary until the students demonstrate their understanding of the task. You must be especially prepared to address questions about the centrality of the L1 in the activity as it is likely that students will be more used to English as the mode of academic communication. As the activity progresses, you and any available instructional assistants move purposefully and actively throughout the classroom, alternating between giving students time to negotiate the task independently and engaging when elements of the task emerge as difficult. In addition, you monitor and comment on the Google Slides both in-class and online, and, when appropriate, bring key in-class or online clarifications to the attention of the entire class. At the final presentation stage, you support the students by demonstrating acceptable audience behavior and even involve them in the assessment process. Following the presentations, you invite students to reflect on the process and offer suggestions for future improvement. Throughout, you must remain cognizant of the fact that many students may have little experience with bilingual activities, digital multimodal tools, public speaking, and formal interpretation; therefore, the time planned for the activity should be as flexible as possible to support students as they progress through the task.

Procedures

After the direct instructional phase, begin the Bilingual Biomes Project by forming groups, introducing overall project goals and procedures. Students should

- pick a biome from their country(ies) to research.
- research the biome and prepare a group presentation for a bilingual audience.
- prepare a Google Slides presentation in a language other than English.
- deliver the presentation first in the language other than English with interpretation to English by one member of the group.

In addition, provide key online resources (available on the companion website for this book) to the students. First, organize the students into homogeneous language groups, if possible, or at least groups in which there is the possibility for translanguaging or transcultural connections to form. In highly multilingual classrooms, this may be a challenge (see Caveats section); however, in most regions, two to five significant language/cultural groups should emerge. In Derek's context, Spanish, Nepali, and Somali were the dominant languages in the classroom, so he created groups for these languages—one Spanish, one Nepali, and two Somali—and divided the three other students who spoke French/Swahili, Wolof/Fulani, and Zomi/Burmese between the two Somali groups. Second, make the project goals and procedures clear by providing a written description of the project and a grading rubric, and presenting an example of the Google Slides document. Third, the students should have ample time to ask questions, and you should anticipate some questions about the L1 presentation, especially when it is the first activity of this type for the students in the class or school environment.

Following this time, plan a number of group work days during which students gain access to Google Slides and begin the project. The specific work includes selecting a biome from their home country, finding appropriate climate data and images about that biome, and writing the slides in their L1. During this time, you and any available assistants support students by providing examples of a high-quality presentation as well as common mistakes to avoid (e.g., yellow font on a white background), facilitating collaborative and constructive group work, and offering solutions to language-specific challenges (e.g., when students are preliterate in their L1). On the presentation days, encourage student presenters to speak clearly and make eye contact and the audience to be active and respectful listeners so as to participate in the concluding question/answer session.

Closing

The activity ends when all the groups have completed and delivered their presentations. The students should also have a question/answer session with the audience after each presentation, and you should provide some general comments/assessment about each presentation publicly if appropriate and instructive for the whole group or in private if preferred. In turn, the students should have the opportunity to provide feedback to you about the activity process for future improvements.

Extensions

This activity could be extended or modified in a number of ways. On the first day, it may be possible to allow students to form their own language/cultural groups, which may address the issue of students without same-language partners more collaboratively. In addition, you can co-construct the assessment rubric with the students and use that for extended peer group discussion following the activity. Beyond the classroom, the activity could bridge into the community by asking the students to create a list of content words in their L1 and English and use that to have a discussion with their parents or other community members. Moreover, parents could be invited to attend the student presentations.

Caveats

As mentioned previously, a significant caveat for this activity is the creation of homogeneous language groups in highly multilingual classrooms. Given the demographics of many regions, it is likely that there will be several students in a class that will share an L1 (e.g., Spanish) but several others might lack a same-language partner. Thus, it is a linguistic and logistical challenge to place these students with other students in a principled manner. Possible solutions might focus on geographic, linguistic, or cultural similarities, but it may be the case that few similarities can be found, in which case students might be grouped based on personality, friendships, or other reasons. The practical challenge is how students will arrange the presentation itself. In Derek's class, each of the students without a same-language partner made a single slide in their own language to incorporate into the larger Somali presentation. This challenge, however, transcended language in that these students' biomes were not necessarily commensurate with the Somali students'; thus, there was some incoherence in the final presentation, but on the other hand at least all students had a chance to present in their L1 about a relevant biome. In general, you should remain focused on the task of helping students to present in their L1; prepare several alternatives for students without same language partners, but also listen to student suggestions.

Connected to the issue of language, you should be prepared for questioning or even resistance from the students to the bilingual task. Students may simply have become more comfortable with using English in school and may need support to reorient to their L1. This may be particularly strong for SLIFEs whose L1 literacy may not be as strong as other students' literacy. For many students, a dramatic shift to L1 academic use may be quite complex and emotional, indirectly forcing them to address elements of their home life, community, and prior educations that may be frustrating or even painful. Thus, you should be prepared to address any discussions or behaviors that may arise as a result.

Finally, depending on the context in which this activity is implemented, you should plan for extended time for students to set up Google accounts, direct instruction in how to create a Google Slide presentation, and provide adequate support and practice with public speaking. In Derek's class, several students required nearly a whole class period setting up their Gmail accounts and accessing Google Drive. Moreover, online collaboration allows students to make changes to other students' work, which can lead to either accidental or purposeful changing/erasing of content. With adolescent students, this may lead to conflict, and you should spend time discussing this collaborative format and be ready to resolve disputes by, for example, restoring a document to a previous version.

Assessment and Evaluation

The project is assessed using the following rubrics (Appendix A) focused on two main areas: (1) creation of the Google Slides document (see Figure 1), and (2) the quality of the presentation see Figure 2).

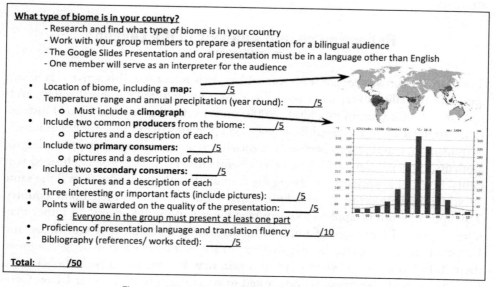

Figure 1. Rubric for the Google Slides presentation.

Bilingual Biome Presentation Project

Name: _____   PD: _____   Date: _____

	1	2	3	4	5
Presentation Quality	Holds no eye contact with audience, as entire report is read from notes. Speaks in low volume and/ or monotonous tone, which causes audience to not be interested.	Displays minimal eye contact with audience, while reading mostly from the notes. Speaks in uneven volume with little or no interest	Consistent use of direct eye contact with audience, but still returns to notes. Speaks with satisfactory variation of volume and inflection	Holds attention of entire audience with the use of direct eye contact, not Looking much at notes. Speaks with high volume and inflection to maintain audience interest	All group members participate in the presentation. Fluid translation. Holds attention of entire audience with the use of direct eye contact, not Looking much at notes. Speaks loud and clearly

Figure 2. Rubric for the oral presentation.

In addition to the formal grade, evaluate the task by distributing a survey (Appendix B) asking the students about what parts they felt were difficult, their feelings about presenting in their L1, and their reflection about the overall task.

It must be stressed that the Derek made no specific effort to assess the students' L1 proficiency or use, either on the Google Slides or in the oral presentation. This prompted one student to ask, "What will you do if I just make something up?," to which Derek responded that it would likely be more effort to make up language than to just do the task as best as possible. In the moment, the student seemed to accept that response, but it is possible that future iterations of this activity may consider ways to assess the L1 without making that an overt or additional stressor for the students.

Reflection on and Analysis of the Lesson

There are two broad areas of reflection and analysis relevant to this activity: language and multimodality. In terms of language, consistent with the empirical and theoretical rationale for Cummins's (2007, 2009) push to destabilize monolingual instructional strategies, this Bilingual Biomes Project provides an example for practitioners, administrators, and researchers who regularly encounter bilingual and multilingual students, especially in super-diverse environments. First, the project engaged students' funds of knowledge by asking them to work with peers who shared the same L1 while drawing on their prior knowledge about a biome in their home country. This approach can be applied to encourage the use of these learners' L1 rather than rejecting their L1 in favor of English. Incorporating their funds of knowledge and L1 into their learning enabled the students to access their prior knowledge, improve their ability to learn a new concept, and gain new knowledge in both their L1 and English. Second, the students were asked to write the content in their L1 on Google Slides and were encouraged to use any available instructional resources, such as bilingual dictionaries (those they had made during the academic year, those officially published in hard copy, or applications such as Google Translate). Doing so allowed the students to engage promptly in higher order cognition and expression in their own languages, rather than struggle with English as the only acceptable intellectual linguistic currency. Third, not only did presenting the content in the L1 and in English allow the students to promote their linguistic awareness of both languages, but they also had the chance to share their bilingual or multilingual abilities with others in classes where their L1 was considered a powerful learning resource.

Throughout, the activity provided validation for the students, particularly those whose L1 language status contributed to their marginalization in other contexts. This outcome was evident in the interviews conducted during and after the project. Most students reported that they found the activity structure advantageous in that its practices deepened their understanding of the concept of biomes in their home country and gave them the chance to practice interpreting their L1 into English, which enabled them to improve their written L1 in an academic setting and speak English before a large audience.

However, not all students participating in this project reported benefitting from the project. This was particularly true of SLIFEs, who demonstrated different levels of L1 proficiency, particularly with regard to academic writing and reading. Their L1 literacy and prior education mitigated the process and outcomes to varying degrees, ranging from the Spanish-speaking group, which completed the task with relative ease, to the one Wolof/Fulani speaker, who was writing in his L1 in an academic context for the first time. In addition to the Wolof/Fulani speaker, all the Nepali speakers and some of the Somali speakers who were pre- or semiliterate in their L1 stated that they had struggled with L1 writing on the Google Slides and therefore had no choice but to rely on Google Translate for English to L1 translation. Moreover, the problem of scripts arose for the Nepali and Zomi/Burmese-speaking students

Desert

A desert is a place that is very dry.
alarya nane nocom cow too

In the desert, there is not a lot of rain.

Alarya goto tobota.

Figure 3. The sole slide created by the Wolof/Fulani-speaking student. The student wrote in Fulani in this activity despite having no formal literacy training in his L1; moreover, the student could not use Google Translate to check his work as both Wolof and Fulani are not available.

သဲကန္တာရ (Desert)

အရှေ့ယီမင်
သဲကန္တာရအများစုဟာအာရှဗျေသဲကန္တာရတဆင်စ
ဆင်းကြေ၏ (ကမ္ဘာ့ဒုတိယအကြီးဆုံးသဲကန္တာရ)
သို့ အဘယ်မှာရှိသဲကန္တာရဖြစ်ပါတယ်။
အလွန်လူ့အနည်းငယ်ကဤနရောတွင်အသက်ရှင်သည်
အတွင်းဒါဟာ
အချည်းနီးသဲရပ်ကွက်အဖစ်ရည်ညွှန်းသည်။
နှင့်အတွက်ရေရိယာအားဖြင့်ရဲစဆာန်များနားများကို
အဘယ်သူ့ဖန့်ရှိခါဖြစ်လျက်ရှိပါသည်။

Most of eastern Yemen is the desert, where it slopes into the Arabian Desert (the second largest desert in the world). It is referred to as the Empty Quarter as very few people live here. There are the occasional nomads who herd animals through the area in the spring.

Figure 4. The sole slide created by the Zomi/Burmese-speaking student. This student chose to write in Burmese rather than her L1 Zomi because her formal education had been primarily in Burmese. However, despite her strong proficiency in academic Burmese, it was difficult to install a Burmese keyboard on the Chromebooks, so she wrote the English text into Google Translate and then copy/pasted into the Google Slides.

Secondary consumers माध्यमिक उपभोक्ताहरु

Dosro Upabhokta

This animal name is Snow Leopard. This animal live in Himalayan region. This animal eat other animal such as tahr.

यो पशु नाम हिम छ चितुवा । यो जनावर बस्ने हिमालय क्षेत्र। यो जनावर खान यस्तो thar अन्य पशु ।

Figure 5. One of a number of slides from the Nepali-speaking students. The students wrote in English and used Google Translate to create the Nepali text, but had difficulty installing a Nepali keyboard on the Chromebooks.

in that it was difficult to install non-English keyboards on the Chromebooks and, even if that had been successful, the students were unfamiliar with the L1 keyboard maps. In contrast, the Spanish-speaking groups were able to write directly in their L1 and/or easily use Google Translate, Wikipedia, or other online sources to create

Engaging Research: Transforming Practices for the High School Classroom

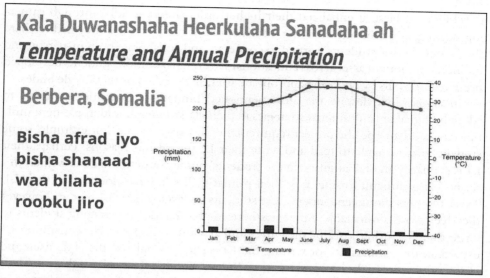

Kala Duwanashaha Heerkulaha Sanadaha ah
Temperature and Annual Precipitation

Berbera, Somalia

Bisha afrad iyo bisha shanaad waa bilaha roobku jiro

Figure 6. One of a number of slides from the Somali-speaking students. Some students wrote the Somali text on their own and others used Google Translate.

LOS PRODUCTORES

HADA DUSTER

El Hada Duster tiene las bolas de hojaldre - naranja rosado que pueden ser de hasta 2 pulgadas de diámetro . Estos pueden florecer durante todo el año , pero sobre todo en febrero a mayo

FAIRY DUSTER

The Fairy Duster has pink-orange puff balls that can be up to 2 inches in diameter. These can bloom all year round but mostly in February through May

Figure 7. One of a number of slides from the Spanish-speaking students. The students generally wrote the Spanish text on their own but were able to compare their texts with online tools.

their slides. Figures 3–7 demonstrate this range of L1 literacy abilities as reflected in the final presentation slides.

Overall, although some students might not have benefited from the biliteracy practices as much as the others, they showed understanding of the biome concept by presenting what they were required to. In addition, the online process enriched the learning environment by offering students various opportunities for skill development. First, it enhanced their higher order thinking skills through gathering, sorting, and critically selecting information. Second, because they had to share the Google Slides, students learned to cooperate and collaborate both in-person and online, an important asset across educational settings. In addition, students developed presentation skills by choosing appropriate font, size, and color on Google Slides.

In conclusion, despite the aforementioned limitations, practitioners eager to adopt bilingual or multilingual strategies in their classrooms should implement multiple and student-specific project requirements and assessments. For example, some students may struggle to read and write their L1 for various reasons. Perhaps their L1 is primarily an oral language in the students' home country, the L1 is written in a script that is difficult for them, or their primary schooling has not been in their L1. Thus, teachers should encourage these students to develop their L1 literacy however they feel most comfortable. Strategies here might include encouraging students to write their L1 using a script they are familiar with (e.g., English), consulting L1 experts in the community, or writing the L1 script sparingly on the slide itself and elaborating more in the oral presentation. Indeed, because the students draw on their L1 and funds of knowledge, inviting parents or community members to take part in the project would improve the availability of instructional resources.

Even though some challenges remain, overall, the students benefited from the Bilingual Biomes Project. Some students (e.g., Nepali speakers and a Wolof speaker) had a chance to write in their home languages for the first time in a U.S. school setting, locate literacy resources, and develop home-language vocabulary. Others expanded their L1 abilities by interpreting simultaneously; giving an academic presentation and learning obscure, scientific, or specific vocabulary; and noticing translanguaging connections. If the teacher had implemented the activity earlier in the year and employed this general pedagogy across the curriculum in creative ways, this approach could be a powerful tool for supporting the increasingly super-diverse students in the United States or beyond.

The appendixes and additional resources for this chapter are available at www.tesol.org/practices-highschool.

Brian Seilstad is a doctoral candidate in the Department of Teaching and Learning at the Ohio State University, Columbus, Ohio, USA, with research interest in multicultural and equity studies in education.

Derek Braun is a member of the ESL Department in Columbus City Schools, Ohio, USA, currently teaching Biology and Anatomy at Beechcroft High School.

Somin Kim is a doctoral student in the Department of Teaching and Learning at the Ohio State University, Columbus, Ohio, USA, with a focus on multilingual English learners' language and literacy practices in classroom settings.

Min-Seok Choi is a doctoral candidate in the department of Teaching and Learning at the Ohio State University, Columbus, Ohio, USA, with research interests in second/academic language socialization, ethnography of language and literacy, discourse analysis, and language ideology.

References

Blommaert, J. (2013). *Ethnography, superdiversity and linguistic landscapes: Chronicles of complexity*. Bristol, England: Multilingual Matters.

Cummins, J. (2007). Rethinking monolingual instructional strategies in multilingual classrooms. *Canadian Journal of Applied Linguistics, 10*(2), 221–240.

Cummins, J. (2009). Multilingualism in the English-language classroom: Pedagogical considerations. *TESOL Quarterly, 43*, 317–321. doi:10.1002/j.1545-7249.2009 .tb00171.x

Echevarría, J. J., Vogt, M. J., & Short, D. J. (2012). *Making content comprehensible for English learners: The SIOP model* (4th ed.). Boston, MA: Pearson.

García, O., Johnson, S. I., & Seltzer, K. (2017). *The translanguaging classroom: Leveraging student bilingualism for learning*. Philadelphia, PA: Caslon.

Lewis, L., & Gray, L. (2016). Programs and services for high school English learners in public school districts: 2015–16. Washington, DC: National Center for Education Statistics.

Ohio Department of Education. (2015, June). *Ohio English language proficiency standards*. Columbus, OH: Author.

Ohio Department of Education. (2011). Ohio's new learning standards: Science standards. Retrieved from http://education.ohio.gov/getattachment/Topics /Learning-in-Ohio/Science/ScienceStandards.pdf.aspx?lang=en-US

Ohio Department of Education. (2018). Ohio English Language Proficiency Assessment (OELPA). Retrieved from http://education.ohio.gov/Topics/Testing /Ohio-English-Language-Proficiency-Assessment-OELPA

Otheguy, R., García, O., & Reid, W. (2015). Clarifying translanguaging and deconstructing named languages: A perspective from linguistics. *Applied Linguistics Review, 6*(3), 281–307. doi:10.1515/applirev-2015-0014

Suárez-Orozco, C., Gaytán, F. X., Bang, H. J., Pakes, J., O'Connor, E., & Rhodes, J. (2010). Academic trajectories of newcomer immigrant youth. *Developmental Psychology, 46*(3), 602–618. doi:10.1037/a0018201

Valentino, R. A., & Reardon, S. F. (2015). Effectiveness of four instructional programs designed to serve English learners: Variation by ethnicity and initial English proficiency. *Educational Evaluation and Policy Analysis, 37*(4), 612–637.

Yi, Y., & Angay-Crowder, T. (2016). Multimodal pedagogies for teacher education in TESOL. *TESOL Quarterly, 50*, 988–998. doi:10.1002/tesq.326

Transforming Language and Content in Science Learning for Secondary English Learners

Francine M. Johnson, Cynthia Lima, Jorge Solís

Introduction

The lesson plan described in this chapter is designed for a high school science lesson about climate change and implements the use of accountable talk (AT) to promote academic discourse development for secondary English learners (ELs). The lesson plan draws from the Next Generation Science Standards (NGSS), endorsed by the National Research Council, which focus on science practices needed for 21st-century learning and workplace skills (NGSS Lead States, 2013). To ensure engagement with authentic science literacy practices, this lesson plan focuses on NGSS Practice 2, the creation and use of models, and NGSS Practice 7, engaging in arguments with the use of evidence. We utilize the "Climate Rapid Overview and Decision Support" simulator, also known as C-ROADS (an online climate change simulator that allows students to see how different variables affect climate change in various regions), to assist students in drawing conclusions about the impact of different variables on climate change. We chose this simulator because it allows for hands-on engagement; provides excellent graphs to serve as visual support for ELs; uses models and literacy practices to build conceptual understandings; and can be used in English or Spanish, thus allowing many ELs to use their full linguistic repertoires when making meaning.

In this chapter, we propose that AT can be used productively in science classrooms because it addresses how to promote purposeful student interaction by apprenticing ELs to disciplinary Discourse communities. Explicit and tiered scaffolding to academic discourse and literacy practices are critical forms of support for secondary ELs.

Though the anchor article (Ardasheva, Howell, & Vidrio Magaña, 2016) focused on the use of AT in mathematics, this chapter proposes that AT can be implemented in all curricular content areas with ELs with the appropriate adaptations to particular classroom contexts. We adapted the research to create a science lesson plan that incorporates NGSS science practices related to the use of models in the classroom and the use of AT as a means for all students to become active members in the development of scientific discourse practices (i.e., scientific explanations, argumentation, use of models, etc.). We built the lesson plan on a perspective of modeling in science education, which allows students to represent scientific phenomena through models that are shared verbally and require the use of specialized disciplinary symbols or other representations (Gilbert, 2004). Adaptations to the lesson also focused on leveraging AT practices that provided opportunities for authentic and dialogic interactions, complex sense-making and reasoning, and the synergistic integration of language and content learning (Michaels, O'Connor, & Resnick, 2008; Stoddart, Pinal, Latzke, & Canaday, 2002; Wells, 1999). The AT approach helps teachers structure and manage critical language and content learning opportunities in what Walqui (2006) refers to as "joint activities that focus on matters of shared interest" (p. 160). These approaches suggest that students need authentic opportunities to interact with both students and teachers to maximize learning.

AT approaches in science, technology, engineering, and mathematics (STEM) subjects can offer a language-rich and research-based alternative for countering current approaches to socializing students to academic discourses, which remain largely didactic, teacher centered, and one dimensional. Traditional classroom interaction patterns, like the initiation-response-evaluation (I-R-E) format (Mehan, 1979), continue to dominate in high school classrooms despite the growing evidence of the positive and significant benefits of peer-mediated interaction for ELs (Pyle, Pyle, Lignugaris/Kraft, Duran, & Akers, 2017). In classrooms with I-R-E dominated patterns, the teacher remains the driving voice that initiates and evaluates classroom talk. In this traditional didactic format, students are not expected to be legitimate interlocutors as they are often not shown how to listen to each other and how to respond or add on to the contributions of their peers (Cazden, 2001). In I-R-E, student contributions are often short and show recitation of knowledge (Gallimore & Tharp, 1990). The I-R-E format can be useful, when used sparingly, as a means to support learning by providing feedback (Gibbons, 2002; Gallimore & Tharp, 1990). However, ELs need supportive opportunities to participate in more dialogic interactions to become socialized to content-specific discourse practices and to develop their academic identities.

ELs spend the majority of their instructional time with mainstream teachers (Bunch, 2010). Though student diversity is increasing, the majority of U.S. teachers tend to be White, monolingual speakers of English (Bunch, 2010). Additionally, most mainstream teachers have received little to no professional development or preparation to effectively provide instruction to ELs (Faltis, Arias, & Ramírez-Marín, 2010; Solís & Bunch, 2016). Though EL struggles at the elementary and secondary levels are similar, secondary ELs face the additional challenge of the linguistic demands of academic work that is increasingly linked to particular content areas (Bunch, 2010). Secondary ELs are asked to demonstrate their learning through a variety of academic literacy genres; often, the expected literacy tasks, without appropriate supports, are beyond the ELs' language proficiency (Solís & Bunch, 2016). Solís and Bunch (2016) state, "integrating literacy and language instruction with content-area instruction addresses the need to teach EL disciplinary-specific literacy tasks *without* denying them access to participating in the authentic practices at the heart of the discipline" (p. 24). It is important to integrate content and literacy instruction so that students can develop their academic literacy and increase content knowledge. Bunch (2013) contends that teachers must "purposefully enact opportunities for the development of language and literacy in and through teaching the core curricular content, understandings, and activities that teachers are responsible for (and, hopefully, excited about) teaching in the first place" (p. 298). This means that teachers must provide opportunities for students to develop their academic language and literacy through carefully structured activities (promoting interaction and engagement) while maintaining rigor by teaching the core curriculum.

Synopsis of Original Research

Ardasheva, Y., Howell, P. B., & Vidrio Magaña, M. (2016). Accessing the classroom discourse community through accountable talk: English learners' voices. *TESOL Journal, 7,* 667–699. doi:10.1002 /tesj.237

Ardasheva et al. (2016) conducted a year-long case study in three middle school mathematics classes to investigate ELs' perspectives regarding AT, which is a structured, discourse-intensive instructional approach. Ardasheva et al. cite Gee's (2014) definition of *Discourse* (with a capital *D*) as the ways of being, saying, and doing. School discourses often reflect the norms of middle and upper-class society "and are associated with power, prestige, and access to social goods, including material goods, status, and solidarity" (p. 668). Many ELs enter school with a set of discourse patterns that are different from those at school. Differences in school are often seen as problematic and differences in discourse often lead to exclusion from academic communities of practice, ultimately undermining ELs' chances to succeed. Therefore, it is essential for ELs to have opportunities to participate and practice in the academic discourse of school to gain entrance to that community of practice. There is much academic research about ELs' development of academic language, but there is little research that focuses on instructional methods to increase ELs' integration into school-based discourse communities. Research on EL student perspectives is even more limited. Ardasheva et al.'s study, using AT, attempted to address this gap in the research.

AT is based on three principles: (1) accountability to the learning community; (2) accountability to standards of reasoning; and (3) accountability to knowledge, developed to assist students in participating in academic discourse practices (Michaels, O'Connor, & Resnick, 2008). These same principles are taken up in the anchor article used for this lesson. To demonstrate accountability to the learning community, students must actively listen and respond to the contributions of others. Accountability to standards of reasoning is demonstrated by providing logical and reasonable connections between claims and conclusions. Accountability to knowledge includes talk that is supported by evidence for claims and conclusions (for a taxonomy of AT dimensions, see Appendix A, available on the companion website for this book).

Providing students the opportunity to learn D/discourse features while navigating the school culture across and beyond academic subject matter contexts is necessary for gaining access to the culture and language of power. Gee's (1989) theory of discourse puts forth an open-membership hypothesis, which "holds that instructional models a) target both language speakers and language learners; b) focus on developing conscious awareness of the Discourse features, and c) provide means for Discourse verbalization and critical analysis by means of developing a meta-language" (p. 9). In their research investigation, Ardasheva et al. (2016) attempted to test the open-membership hypothesis by incorporating EL students' perspectives on the use of AT.

The study (Ardasheva et al., 2016) occurred with one seventh-grade mathematics teacher who was trained in AT and her three math classes, comprising 68 students. One class was advanced placement (AP) and two were comprehensive math classes. The researchers relied on student interviews as the main data source, and they used approximately 2 hours of teacher interviews and classroom observations for data triangulation and contextualization of findings. Observations were conducted at the beginning and near the end of the school year to provide contextualization of findings.

Twenty-one ELs (10 female and 11 male) participated in the study. The average age of student participants was 13. All students participated in the focus group interviews and three students (two Spanish-speaking females and one Spanish-speaking male) participated in individual interviews. Eighteen students were enrolled in the comprehensive math class and three were enrolled in the AP level mathematics class. On average, the ELs in the study have attended U.S. schools for 3.9 years, and their English proficiency levels ranged from early intermediate to advanced. The teacher in the study had 2 years of teaching experience. She had a bachelor's degree in education, but she had no formal preparation in teaching ELs. She learned about AT through direct instruction and modeling in her education courses and through professional development.

Based on EL interviews, three themes emerged regarding the implementation of AT in the Ardasheva et al. (2016) study. The researchers report on secondary students' perceptions of AT as a means for helping them feel more prepared and confident in their ability to participate in academic interactions. Specifically, they reported that AT improved the quality of classroom interaction, expanded learning opportunities, and left students feeling empowered to get ahead in school and life. Students expressed increased ability to use mathematical language and practices and that AT taught them "proper conversation skills" for the classroom and beyond (p. 685). Importantly, students perceived AT as a means of "treating everyone as equal" (p. 686) and as a way to bring everyone together, offering a "friendlier" environment. For expanded learning opportunities, students believed that AT allowed them to share mathematical understandings while learning new words and that it increased the opportunity to teach others. When students discussed how AT provides an opportunity to get ahead in school and life, they mentioned how it is helpful to them in other classes as well because they know how to choose their words wisely and share information with others, and they saw it as an opportunity to help them earn better grades. One EL stated that when using AT, "it is like you are higher class" (p. 689). Interestingly, this study was conducted with students in mainstream and upper academic tracks, and all students cited the personal benefits of AT. However, higher track students were more likely to report an awareness of the benefits of AT for their long-term career goals. This serves as a gentle reminder that AT works for all students, and teachers need to be explicit about disciplinary and classroom discourse practices to ensure that all students (regardless of academic placement or purported abilities) can be socialized into academic communities of practice.

With the increased diversity of learners in U.S. public schools, teachers need to be equipped to provide ELs with quality and rigorous learning opportunities in science. Teachers find themselves in need of instructional practices that facilitate student engagement while integrating content and language instruction. Through the lens of EL perspectives, this study (Ardasheva et al., 2016) corroborated the open-membership hypothesis, suggesting that explicitly teaching school-based Discourse may help language minority students. In turn, students will gain access to school culture while participating in more student-to-student interactions.

Rationale

Ardasheva et al.'s (2016) research acknowledges the value of research related to ELs' academic and language outcomes while pointing out the dearth of research examining instructional methods that advance ELs' integration into school-based Discourse communities (e.g., academic and disciplinary discourses). Moreover, this work is innovative because the AT model has not been studied widely with ELs. Furthermore, this research provides a unique example of how teachers can support ELs' integration into school-based Discourse communities by attending to students' sense-making in STEM fields. In the following lesson, we present an instructional practice that shows promise for secondary educators by modeling how to work productively with secondary ELs in STEM subjects.

Lesson Plan

Lesson Plan Title	Climate Patterns
Grade/Subject Area	Grades 9–12; Science
Duration	≈ 3 hours
Proficiency Levels	All levels
Content and Language Objectives	Students will be able to • use a climate change model to design an environmental initiative for their city. (Content) • engage in accountable talk to support the construction of scientific knowledge (climate change). (Language)

(continued on next page)

Lesson Plan *(continued)*	
Alignment to Standards	**English Language Proficiency Standards** (CCSSO, 2014) • *ELP 9-12.1*: Construct meaning from oral presentations and literary and informational text through grade-appropriate listening, reading and viewing. • *ELP 9-12.4*: Construct grade appropriate written and oral claims and support them with reasoning and evidence. (Connected to EP3: Construct valid arguments from evidence and critique the reasoning of others; EP5: Build upon the ideas of others and articulate his or her own ideas when working collaboratively; SP7: Engage in argument from evidence.) • *ELP 9-12.6*: Analyze and critique the arguments of others orally and in writing. (Connected to EP3: Construct valid arguments from evidence and critique the reasoning of others; SP7: Engage in argument from evidence.) **Next Generation Science Standards** (NGSS Lead States, 2013) *High School; Practice 2 (Developing and Using Models)* • Develop, revise, and/or use a model based on evidence to illustrate and/or predict the relationships between systems or between components of a system. • Develop and/or use multiple types of models to provide mechanistic accounts and/or predict phenomena, and move flexibly between model types based on merits and limitations. *High School; Practice 7 (Engaging in Arguments With Evidence)* • Respectfully provide and/or receive critiques on scientific arguments by probing reasoning and evidence, challenging ideas and conclusions, responding thoughtfully to diverse perspectives, and determining additional information required to resolve contradictions. • Construct, use and/or present an oral and written argument or counter-arguments based on data and evidence.
Outcomes	Students will • create and use models to represent conceptual understandings. • propose and defend an environmental initiative to reduce carbon.

Materials	• Internet access
	• Appendixes B–H (available on the companion website for this book)
	  — K-W-L chart (Appendix B)
	  — Word wall handout (Appendix C)
	  — Graphic organizer for "Jigsaw" activity (Appendix D)
	  — C-ROADS assumptions handout (Appendix E)
	  — Sample C-ROADS images (Appendix F)
	  — Accountable talk student bookmarks (Appendix G)
	  — Rubric (Appendix H)
	• Poker chips
	• Chart paper

Highlighted Teaching Strategies

This lesson utilizes the following teaching strategies:

1. K-W-L chart to show what is already known, what the student wants to learn, and what was learned (Reiss, 2012, p. 58)

2. Think-pair-share (Echevarría, Vogt & Short, 2014, p. 198)

3. Jigsaw activity (Echevarría, Vogt, and Short, 2014, p. 46)

4. Previewing vocabulary

5. Use of visuals to support comprehension (Echevarría, Vogt, & Short, 2014)

Procedures

In this lesson, you will pose essential questions such as:

- How do changes in different Earth subsystems affect climate change?

- How do variations in human activity affect climate change (the production of different kinds of pollutants, including greenhouse gases)?

- What are the possible sources of fossil fuel emissions that humans can try to reduce?

- How do potential reductions in carbon emissions impact climate change?

Building background (20 minutes)

Begin the lesson by building background. Have students complete a K-W-L chart (Appendix B) about climate change, individually completing the K (What do I want to know?) column and the W (What do I want to know?) columns individually. Next, lead the students in a think-pair-share activity by asking them to discuss the K and W columns with a partner. After students have had ample time to discuss with a partner, pull the discussion back to the whole class, asking students what they have in the K and W columns while writing it on chart paper that is displayed for all to see. Finally, preview some key vocabulary to be used throughout the lesson by all students, including: *variables, model, fossil fuels, deforestation, afforestation, carbon emissions, emit, impact*. These words (and others that might come up in the unit of study) will be incorporated into the word wall (Appendix C) that students can reference at any time.

Contextualization (20 minutes)

Show students "Climate Change—a student demonstration" (www.teachertube.com /video/climate-change-a-student-demonstration-192686; link directly from the companion website for this book) so they can see how some students created a model for global warming and climate change. Before the video begins, equally divide the class into groups of three and assign each group member a number (1, 2, or 3); students of each number will be the "experts" for their corresponding question. While this grouping purports to be random, you should take into consideration language background and proficiency. Assign a focus question to each number: (1) What variables did the students include in the model? (2) What relationships among variables does the model describe? (3) What would be some of the possible limitations of the model in terms of being able to explain global warming and climate change?

Pause the video at specific points to give students time to write down information that corresponds to their assigned question in their graphic organizer (Appendix D). After the video has stopped, give students in like (expert) groups 3–4 minutes to compare what they wrote down. Next, have them return to their home group (containing a 1, 2, and 3) and report on their findings. Ask for responses to the questions and complete the graphic organizer (all questions) on chart paper or on the computer projection. Ask the contextualization questions to the class and create a three-column chart to record student responses.

C-ROADS introduction and application (45–50 minutes)

At this point in the lesson, the students have analyzed the video of the model of global warming/global change and have identified some of the variables and relationships. Begin to introduce the C-ROADS simulator (www.climateinteractive.org /tools/c-roads; link directly from the companion website for this book). C-ROADS is a great use of technology for ELs because it provides visuals to support comprehension and uses key vocabulary in context, and the simulator can be used in English or in Spanish, allowing for students to move fluidly between their language of ideas and language of display (Bunch, 2013). Frame the use of the models with a purpose, and tell students, "The objective is to come up with an environmental initiative for our city to improve air quality and decrease the temperature." The model should show changes that are feasible within the city budget (or can include other conditions). In this way, the students explore the C-ROADS with a purpose.

To be sure students realize that we need to consider other models as well, provide a handout of a condensed/modified version of the assumptions of the C-ROADS model (Appendix E). (This will support later discussion about what would happen if we change some of the assumptions.) Demonstrate how the C-ROADS simulator can calculate changes in temperature (global warming) dependent on variables (different emissions). Encourage students to observe the impact of different emissions variables as well as how various regional variables can impact carbon emissions. After providing data and resources from the Environmental Protection Agency, include some questions to guide students' explorations, such as: How much can you reduce your individual emissions? Will this reduction have a significant impact on the Earth's temperature? These guiding questions allow students the opportunity to make the learning more personally relevant after adjusting given variables that are available in the C-ROADS simulator. See Appendix F for example charts and graphs that students might see by adjusting variables related to climate change. Ask for student predictions, model the input of data, and allow students to see the results and make a conclusion.

In small groups (three to four students), have students go to computers to use the C-ROADS website, entering data for their specific type of emission to see how their data affects the temperature. Have them create a graph generated by the simulation to show their results, and then have students create a cause-effect statement, such as: By increasing _____ by _____ increments, the temperature increased _____. By decreasing _____ by _____ increments, the temperature decreased _____.

Group presentations (30 minutes)

After creating their summary statements, the student groups present their findings to the class, using key terms (which have been supported and developed throughout the lesson). At the end, they should allow time for student responses and questions.

Finding consensus (15 minutes)

Finally, based on student group findings and presentations, each group will prioritize the ways in which we (as a society) can reduce carbon emissions. Each group must explain with evidence how they prioritized initiatives, using chart paper to display their plan/initiative. While in groups, students must use AT to come to consensus, using their AT bookmarks (Appendix G) for support.

Discussion (25 minutes)

Provide instruction and model how to make a scientific argument, which must contain three elements: the claim, evidence, and reasoning (McNeill & Pimentel, 2010). Next, provide a few more models and have students use a rubric to assess the effectiveness of the scientific arguments provided in the models. The Lawrence Hall of Science has provided video samples of oral arguments, examples of written arguments, and rubrics that can be used to help guide this section of the instruction (www.argumentationtoolkit.org/session-23.html). Have students discuss their evaluations of the claims (using the argumentation rubric) with a peer or small group of three. After group discussions have occurred, host a whole-class discussion, and if the model does not provide evidence to support the claim and/or is not within the city's budget, students must identify what was needed in the scientific argument to be more effective. Give students time in their original groups to work on their arguments and presentations to be sure they adhere to the three elements: claim, evidence, and reasoning.

Moving desks or tables so that groups can sit in a semicircle or circle, students will present their initiatives and receive feedback from peers. Using the principles of AT, students should use evidence, accepted standards of reasoning, and accountability to the community to engage in discussion. To ensure all students participate, have students use poker chips to "spend" a poker chip each time they make a verbal contribution to discussion, pushing the poker chip to the front of their table or desk space. These poker chips will be used to quantify contributions and hold students accountable to participation. Use a the AT rubric (Appendix H) to note what types of conversational moves are made by students and to see how well students are able to engage in science practices and scientific discourse.

Closing (15 minutes)

After the lesson, students complete the L column of the K-W-L chart, writing what they have learned. After writing it down individually, they should turn and talk with a partner about what they learned. Also, have students complete a 3-2-1 exit ticket: They write three things they learned, two things that were interesting, and one relationship between issues of global warming and other Earth systems.

Extensions

The relationship between issues of global warming and other Earth systems that students come up with on their exit tickets leads to future extensions of the lesson.

Caveats

Like any instructional routine, AT requires practice and consistency. You will need to adapt it to your own disciplinary discourse needs, model it, and provide explicit feedback and assessment of students' ability to conform to the three forms of accountability. Additionally, you should probably work on adding language functions as time goes on. For example, at first, students might practice listening to one another. Then, they might practice respectfully asking questions or challenging. Then, they might practice responses. Within these moves, they might focus on sentence stems each day or each week that enable them to make even more conversational moves. This is not an overnight process; it takes sustained effort and dedication. This lesson assumes that teachers have put in time to establish the norms of AT. A video that offers a short professional development for AT is available on YouTube (www.youtube.com /watch?v=AE8BHzPzna8; link directly from the companion website for this book).

Assessment and Evaluation

You may use the completed K-W-L charts and the exit tickets for assessment. We encourage the use of the AT rubric (Appendix H) and the rubrics provided in the argumentation toolkit (www.argumentationtoolkit.org/session-23.html). Though these serve as formal tools for assessment and evaluation, the teacher should be moving around the room throughout the lesson to listen to groups working together to help check for understanding.

Reflection on and Analysis of the Lesson

The TESOL research inspiring this chapter (Ardasheva et al., 2016) shows how the principles of AT can be used to support the academic discourse development of secondary ELs in STEM courses. In this lesson, we adapted AT to work with scientific discourse practices and content objectives. In this case, we specifically focused on NGSS Practice 2 (creating and using models) and NGSS Practice 7 (engaging in arguments with evidence). The lesson highlighted in this chapter is intended to help STEM teachers consider ways of implementing the use of AT to support secondary ELs' content-specific discourse development in a wide variety of contexts. Moreover, the activities and guidelines provided here can be and, in some cases, must be adapted as needed to addresses particular disciplinary discourse practices (biology, chemistry, etc.) and content objectives.

Instructional support of disciplinary discourse practices requires a balance of explicit instruction, modeling scientific practices, and orchestrating language-rich science experiences in the classroom. This lesson attends to this instructional balance through the use of C-ROADS. The goal here is to offer students multiple opportunities to interact with peers while providing, when needed, additional support to ELs (e.g., the use of graphic organizers, sentence stems, word walls, and peer feedback). In addition, authentic assessment activities using rubrics are offered as a tool to capture student comprehension and allow for the adjustment of instruction. The use of rubrics is another way to strengthen language and literacy support in science lessons and for supporting ELs' participation in content-specific discourse practices (Solís & Bunch, 2016). Attending to language functions used in scientific practices (scientific argumentation, using models) offers a dual benefit for ELs: the development of both language skills and science content knowledge.

The appendixes and additional resources for this chapter are available at www.tesol.org/practices-highschool.

Francine M. Johnson is a doctoral student in culture, literacy, and language at the University of Texas San Antonio, Texas, USA, whose research interest is the academic discourse development and literacy practices of secondary ELs.

Cynthia Lima is a lecturer in the Department of Bicultural-Bilingual Students at the University of Texas San Antonio, Texas, USA, whose research is focused on equitable STEM assessment practices for diverse cultural and linguistic populations.

Jorge Solís is an associate professor in the Department of Bicultural-Bilingual Studies at the University of Texas at San Antonio, Texas, USA, whose research interests focus on the intersection of STEM education and literacy for second language learners.

References

Ardasheva, Y., Howell, P. B., & Vidrio Magaña, M. (2016). Accessing the classroom discourse community through accountable talk: English learners' voices. *TESOL Journal, 7,* 667–699. doi:10.1002/tesj.237

Bunch, G. C. (2010). Preparing mainstream secondary content-area teachers to facilitate English language learners' development of academic language. *The Yearbook of the National Society for the Study of Education, 109*(2), 351–383.

Bunch, G. C. (2013). Pedagogical language knowledge: Preparing mainstream teachers for English learners in the new standards era. *Review of Research in Education, 37*(1), 298–341. doi:10.3102/0091732X12461772

Cazden, C. (2001). *Classroom discourse: The language of teaching and learning* (2nd ed.). Portsmouth, NH: Heinemann.

Council of Chief State School Officers (CCSO). (2014). English language proficiency (ELP) standards: With Correspondences to K–12 English Language Arts (ELA), Mathematics, and Science Practices, K–12 ELA Standards, and 6–12 Literacy Standards. Washington, DC: Author. Retrieved from http://www.k12.wa.us /MigrantBilingual/pubdocs/ELP/WA-ELP-Standards-K12.pdf

Echevarría, J., Vogt, M., & Short, D. (2014). *Making content comprehensible for secondary English learners: The SIOP Model* (2nd ed.). Upper Saddle River, NJ: Pearson.

Faltis, C., Arias, M. B., & Ramírez-Marín, F. (2010). Identifying relevant competencies for secondary teachers of English learners. *Bilingual Research Journal, 33*(3), 307–328. doi:10.1080/15235882.2010.529350

Gallimore, R., & Tharp, R. G. (1990). Teaching mind in society: teaching, schooling, and literate discourse. In L. C. Moll (Ed.), *Vygotsky and education: Instructional implications and applications of sociohistorical psychology* (pp. 175–205). New York, NY: Cambridge University Press.

Gee, J. (2012). *Social linguistics and literacies: Ideology in discourses* (4th ed.). New York, NY: Routledge.

Gee, J. (2014). *An introduction to discourse analysis: Theory and method* (4th ed.). New York, NY: Routledge.

Gibbons, P. (2002). *Scaffolding language, scaffolding learning: Teaching second language learners in the mainstream classroom.* Portsmouth, NH: Heinemann.

Gilbert, J. K. (2004). Models and modelling: Routes to more authentic science education. *International Journal of Science and Mathematics Education, 2*(2), 115–130.

McNeill, K. L., & Pimentel, D. S. (2010). Scientific discourse in three urban classrooms: The role of the teacher in engaging high school students in argumentation. *Science Education, 94*(2), 203–229.

Mehan, H. (1979). *Learning lessons: Social organization in the classroom.* Cambridge, MA: Harvard University Press.

Michaels, S., O'Connor, C., & Resnick, L. B. (2008). Deliberative discourse idealized and realized: Accountable talk in the classroom and in civic life. *Studies in Philosophy and Education, 27*(4), 283–297. doi:10.1007/s11217-007-9071-1

NGSS Lead States. (2013). *Next Generation Science Standards: For states, by states.* Washington, DC: The National Academies Press. Retrieved from http://www.nextgenscience.org/

Pyle, D., Pyle, N., Lignugaris/Kraft, B., Duran, L., & Akers, J. (2017). Academic effects of peer-mediated interventions with English language learners: A research synthesis. *Review of Educational Research, 87*(1), 103–133.

Reiss, J. (2012). *Content strategies for English language learners: Teaching for academic success in secondary schools* (2nd ed.). Boston, MA: Pearson.

Solís, J., & Bunch, G. C. (2016). Responsive approaches for teaching English learners in secondary science classrooms: Foundations of the SSTELLA framework. In E. G. Lyon, S. Tolbert, J. Solís, & G. C. Bunch (Eds.), *Secondary science teaching for English learners: Developing supportive and responsive learning contexts for sense-making and language development* (pp. 21–48). Lanham, MD: Rowman & Littlefield.

Stoddart, T., Pinal, A., Latzke, M., & Canaday, D. (2002). Integrating inquiry science and language development for English language learners. *Journal of Research in Science Teaching, 39*(8), 664–687.

Walqui, A. (2006). Scaffolding instruction for English language learners: A conceptual framework. *International Journal of Bilingual Education and Bilingualism, 9*(2), 159–180. doi:10.1080/13670050608668639

Wells, G. (1999). *Dialogic inquiry: Towards a socio-cultural practice and theory of education.* Cambridge, England: Cambridge University Press.

On Shaky Grounds: Teaching Earthquake Science to English Learners Through Guided Visualization

Alandeom W. Oliveira, Luciana de Oliveira, Carla Meskill

Introduction

This chapter examines a group of high school teachers' engagement with "Guided Visualization: Promoting ELL Science Literacies Through Images" (Oliveira & Weinburgh, 2016), a TESOL text that calls on instructors to more carefully consider their use of visuals in supporting English learners (ELs) when designing and implementing content-language integrated science lessons. Rather than treating visuals as self-evident (transparent) and inherently helpful to ELs, teachers are encouraged to adopt a "guided visualization" approach whereby ELs' engagement with scientific imagery (illustrations, diagrams, graphs, etc.) is systematically scaffolded through pedagogical strategies, such as simplified visual input and word walls. Such an approach to classroom discussion of complex and abstract scientific imagery, it is argued, can help prevent ELs from experiencing cognitive overload (excessively high mental load or effort).

We begin with a synopsis of our previous research on science teachers' visual pedagogies and the demands that classroom discussion of visual representations place on ELs in secondary science classes. After that, attention shifts to a lesson on earthquake waves entitled "Interpreting the Reference Table P and S Wave Graph," which was codeveloped and cotaught by a team of three high school teachers—Kate (an earth science teacher), Dorothy (an English as a second language [ESL] teacher), and Nora (an ESL preservice teacher)[1]—subsequent to their engagement with our work on guided visualization during a year-long program of professional development. They taught at an urban school in upstate New York known historically for its textile industry.

The lesson was designed to visually scaffold students' understandings of earthquake waves and their ability to read and interpret P and S wave charts. Its main

---

[1] All teacher names are pseudonyms.

objectives were for students to use the P and S wave time travel graph to determine lag time, distance, and origin time. To this end, the teachers incorporated a variety of visual supports (Slinky toys, cross-sectional diagrams of the Earth, a diagram of a geological fault, a YouTube clip of earthquakes, a beaker of water with a pencil to show refraction) and pedagogies (whole-class discussion of images, pair-and-share, exit ticket). The teachers set out to use visuals to demonstrate terminology in a Regents Earth Science class (leading to a standardized state examination) with 27 students, including four ELs (two Spanish speakers from Puerto Rico and two Mandarin speakers from China). As the teachers stated when describing their approach to supporting ELs in science, "Visuals, visuals, visuals!" We close with an examination of the teachers' reflections on the lesson and recommendations regarding the use of visuals in supporting ELs in science.

Synopsis of Original Research

Oliveira, A. W., & Weinburgh, M. H. (2016). Guided visualization: Promoting ELL science literacies through images. In L. C. de Oliveira (Ed.), *The Common Core State Standards for literacy in history/social studies, science, and technical subjects for English language learners: Grades 6–12* (pp. 91–106). Alexandria, VA: TESOL Press.

In the anchor research study, Oliveira and Weinburgh (2016) examined the image-centered pedagogical strategies adopted by two high school science teachers to visually support ELs in content-language integrated classrooms, classrooms where emphasis is equally given to content (in this case science) and language learning (in this case English). Both teachers were experienced; had received professional development, such as the Sheltered Instruction Observation Protocol model training; and were in the process of aligning their classroom practices with the Common Core State Standards for literacy in science and technical subjects.

A central premise of the anchor study is that, when providing ELs with pictorial support, teachers use specific strategies to prevent cognitive overload and promote germane load (optimized working memory load). When students experience cognitive overload, they feel overwhelmed and have problems processing curricular information. In the case of ELs, mental overload can be associated with language as well as content. When engaged with scientific imagery, ELs can experience cognitive overload as a result of an excessively high linguistic load (mental effort due to language) as well as an excessively high conceptual load (mental effort due to content). Potential for cognitive overload is particularly high when ELs are asked to transform texts into visuals (plot or diagram textually encoded content) as well as convert visuals into texts (verbally decode visual representations). Such tasks present conceptual and linguistic demands because students need to possess both conceptual knowledge and communication skills to be able to produce, interpret, and transpose scientific information across visual and textual formats (Sweller, 2010).

Oliveira and Weinburgh's (2016) study describes how two high school teachers made systematic use of pictorial representations (diagrams, word walls, etc.) in ways that helped prevent EL cognitive overload. The first teacher strategically sequenced multiple forms of visual representation during a lesson on human reproduction. Her strategy was to provide students with diagrammatic representations of the human reproductive system before showing a PowerPoint slideshow with a series of highly realistic photographs of a dissection she had previously performed on a pregnant bovine uterus. Devoid of gruesome biological details (blood and bodily fluids), the biologically "clean" diagrams were simpler for students to visualize than the highly detailed and realistic photographs that followed. By showing the clean diagrams first, the teacher provided her ELs with simplified visual input through more comprehensible images and promoted student conceptual understanding before describing in words more complex imagery.

The second teacher visually supported ELs during a lesson on geologic time. The teacher first used a word wall to introduce scientific terminology such as *eon*, *era*, *period*, and *epoch* and made it visually accessible to students before asking them to collaboratively create a scale model of the Earth's history with its main eras (Pre-Cambrian, Paleozoic, Mesozoic, and Cenozoic) sequentially organized along an "adding tape" based on relative time. Having this terminology readily accessible through visual inspection of the classroom walls reduced the linguistic load by eliminating the need for students to have to remember on their own a set of specialized terms that were likely unfamiliar to them.

The research study suggests the need for educational opportunities to make science instruction more visual for ELs, and hence more accessible. Visual literacy has the potential to impact student conceptual mastery and language acquisition, as teachers can more strongly embrace the visual mode of communication in science.

Rationale

Though appealing and intuitive at a surface level, visually supporting EL development of language and content in a coherent and truly accommodating manner can be a complex and challenging pedagogical endeavor. To support rather than overload or distract ELs, pedagogical integration of visuals must have a design that is both purposeful and targeted. Such a task requires, among other things, strategic design, thoughtful planning, and intelligent use. This complexity and potential for complication underscore the need for additional research that can shed some light on practical aspects of enacting visualization on school grounds. This is precisely what we set out to accomplish in this chapter. Our hope is to offer teachers practical guidance on how visualization can be effectively put into practice to accommodate ELs in science classrooms.

To help ELs "see" new or unknown vocabulary words and visualize abstract concepts, content teachers can make use of a variety of visual supports, including pictorial and graphic representations (Garrison & Mora, 1999; Gerena & Keiler, 2012; Swanson, 2010; Hite & Evans, 2006); drawings on playgrounds (Young & Marroquin, 2008); "Farmer in the Dell" charts (tables with categories of words that can be combined into sentences; Hansen, 2006) and information organizers, such as process grids (Hansen, 2006); the Frayer model (graphic organizers that include definitions and drawings for individual words; Fisher & Frey, 2008; Graves, August, & Mancilla-Martinez, 2013); incorporation of home language; additional language word pairs into the captions of textbook illustrations (Quigley, Oliveira, Curry, & Buck, 2011); and computer simulations (Meskill, Mossop, & Bates, 1999). Use of these visual supports is supported by theoretical arguments that pictorial representations promote dual-coding of language knowledge—the verbal and visual stimuli are stored in different parts of the brain, which improves ELs' ability to recall linguistic information (Paivio, 1971; Reed, 2010; Sternberg, 2003) and thereby acquire the target language. However, what is often missing from such inquiries is the role of the teacher and the teacher's visual literacy mediating comprehension and acquisition.

For example, research shows that visual communication is culturally specific rather than universal; the imagery used for communication reflects its visual cultures (Sturken & Cartwright, 2009). Members of a cultural group have preferred ways of seeing or looking that may differ from other groups'. Their visual representations of the world (e.g., drawings and paintings) are cultural manifestations of larger societal developments and carry unique cultural meanings. Evidence also exists that individuals from diverse cultures have differing cognitive processing styles (Nisbett, Peng, Choi, & Norenzayan, 2001; Nisbett & Masuda, 2003). For instance, North Americans have been found to be more analytic and pay attention to focal objects sooner and for a longer period than, for example, East Asians, who tend to attend to contextual and background information and look holistically (Chua, Boland, & Nisbett, 2005). Because students' ways of looking depend on their cultural background (i.e., students from different cultures may have different visual styles), teachers need to more closely consider their visual pedagogies and the implications of those pedagogies for ELs.

Science itself has a unique and highly specialized visual culture that favors abstract images in sharp contrast to realistic and contextualized imagery typically found in lay visual communication (Kress & van Leeuwen, 2006). Therefore, lack of familiarity with scientific visuals can hinder rather than facilitate the learning of science content by ELs who are being introduced to such visuals. Students need guidance on how to "see" or notice significant phenomena and interpret meaningful events; these skills are not an innate ability (Goodwin, 1997). To be able to gain information from the complicated perceptual fields of specialized images (e.g., scientific inscriptions), students need to be socialized into seeing only the most important visual features of the system directly relevant to their focus. In other words, students need to learn how to see scientifically (i.e., according to the scientific norms of visual representation). Such an ability cannot be simply taken for granted. This is precisely what motivated our selection of the anchor research study and the lesson plan described next.

Lesson Plan

Our team of three teachers—Kate, Dorothy, and Nora—coplanned and cotaught an earth science lesson. The teachers adopted a coteaching model whereby Kate (earth science instructor) served as the lead teacher of the entire group of students while Dorothy and Nora implemented "teaching on purpose" (Honigsfeld & Dove, 2010) on the side; that is, they provided students with just-in-time support as they circulated the room monitoring students' progress.

Kate identified the topic of interpreting P and S wave time travel graphs as being particularly challenging to ELs because of the difficult vocabulary and abstract concepts involved. Because she had struggled teaching this topic to her ELs in previous years, she was looking for ways to make the content more accessible ("EL friendly"). Moreover, this was an important topic on the Earth Science Regents Exams (New York state standardized examination) that her students would be taking at the end of the school year. As she emphatically told her students, "I have said over, and over, and over: If you folks can read your reference table and use your reference table charts, you will be fine on the Regents Exam."

After being introduced to the notion of guided visualization, the teachers carefully considered several visually rich interventions and pedagogical strategies. For instance, they thought that it was important to provide students with a "visual hook"—a relatable and concrete prompt or cue to engage them in the topic of earthquakes. To do this, they showed a YouTube clip of an earthquake in China because they thought it would be engaging, particularly to their two Chinese-speaking ELs, who would likely relate to its content. Lasting two class periods, the lesson was structured as a sequence of six instructional activities: slinky demonstration, visual hook, guided practice, collaborative practice, wrap-up, and assessment.

Lesson Plan Title	Interpreting the Reference Table P and S Wave Graph
Grade/Subject Area	Grade 9; Earth science
Duration	2 (50-minute) class periods
Proficiency Levels	New York State English As A Second Language Achievement Test (New York State Education Department, 2012a, 2012b): Intermediate*
Content and Language Objectives	Students will be able to • use a P and S wave time travel graph to determine distance to an epicenter. (Content) • extrapolate beyond the graph. (Content) • use superlative and comparative terms to describe the differences between P and S waves to a partner. (Language) • verbally express their understanding of how seismic waves compare. (Language)
Alignment to Standards	**New York State Education Department Physical Setting/Earth Science Core Curriculum** (2013) *Standard 6 Key Idea 5*: Identifying patterns of change is necessary for making predictions about future behavior and conditions.

(continued on next page)

Lesson Plan *(continued)*	
Outcomes	Students will be able to • describe the main characteristics (shape, movement, speed) of each type of earthquake wave. • verbally summarize velocity and distance covered for either the P or S wave using an earthquake chart. • describe the damage caused by recent earthquakes around the world.
Materials	• Slinky toy • Beaker of water and pencil • Internet access (YouTube) • Overhead projector • Student copies of reference table • Student copies of problem worksheet

*Students' English proficiency was assessed with New York State English As A Second Language Achievement Test (NYSESLAT). At the time of this study, this standardized state test identified four levels of proficiency in ESL: Beginner, Intermediate, Advanced, and Proficient. Since then, with the recent adoption of the New Language Arts Progressions by New York State, NYSESLAT has been revised to five levels of proficiency. (New York State Education Department, 2012a, 2012b).

Highlighted Teaching Strategies

To support their ELs, the teachers adopted a teaching approach wherein each instructional activity started with concrete and dynamic visual aids and then gradually shifted in focus to more abstract and still imagery. For instance, during the demonstration, slinky modeling was followed by examination of diagrammatic representations of each type of seismic wave on the overhead project. Further, modeling of refraction with a pencil inside a beaker of water was followed by examination of cross-sectional diagrams of the Earth. Following is a transcript of Kate's demonstration of P and S waves and refraction:

> *Kate:* When we held a slinky to the back of the room and talked about the difference between an S and a P wave. P waves are compressional, so the slinky, we pushed it and pulled and it went back and forth. And it was faster. And S wave was like a snake, so if you think "s" for snake and "s" for solid, because S waves only pass through solids. The two types of waves are P waves and S waves, and S waves cannot pass through the outer core, and Tyler, why is that?
>
> *Tyler:* Because the outer core is liquid.
>
> *Kate:* Like we said earlier, I was showing you the pencil and the beaker of water [holds up the pencil in the beaker of water, and walks among the desks] it refracts, so the pencil actually looks bent, right? And that's refraction, because the speed of light is different than it is in air, so this pencil looks bent [points to the screen, and returns to the front of the room]. When there's an earthquake, the S waves and P waves are sent out from that earthquake, and the P waves, which in this picture

[pointing to the transparency] are pink, get refracted, or bent just like the light does to make that pencil look bent, so they get bent in that outer core.

This practice of visually scaffolding ELs from the concrete to the abstract was repeatedly adopted throughout the lesson, revisiting the concrete with the introduction of each new concept. It culminated during the Visual Hook and Guided Practice phases when, after having watched a highly realistic and contextualized visual representation of an earthquake (a video), students were provided with highly abstract visual representations (line graphs). As the lesson progressed, directly seeing an earthquake in graphic detail gradually shifted to imagining it abstractly as couplets of waves of various speeds whose epicenter could be spatially and temporally "read" from line graphs (Figure 1). Throughout this scaffolding process, the teachers helped their ELs visualize as well as verbalize earthquakes scientifically:

Kate: What I want to do is to show you, because we talked about earthquakes, but we didn't really see the damage that was done. So, I want to show you a video, a very short YouTube clip of damage that was done by an earthquake in China just a month ago, November 2013. Joe, would you mind getting the lights for me? What we really need to be able to do is we need to be able to interpret the P and S wave graph that is in your Reference Table. You have to be able to locate where an earthquake is given information about P and S waves. You also have to figure out when the earthquake occurred. So this [pointing the transparency] is a chart that we need to become very familiar with . . .

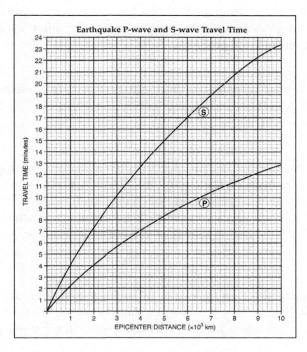

Figure 1. Earthquake P-wave and S-wave travel time.

Procedures

Demonstration

Begin the lesson by modeling the two different types of seismic waves (primary and secondary) with a slinky toy. After visually demonstrating the physical motion of each type of wave, introduce the notion of refraction, which you demonstrate by showing a beaker of water with a pencil inside. Show students a series of diagrams depicting the propagation of waves and cross-sectional diagrams of the Earth as they discuss how P waves can travel through both solids and liquids, whereas S waves can travel only through solids (because of refraction).

Visual hook

Show the YouTube video of a Chinese earthquake. "Earthquake rescue continues in China's Gansu province" (www.youtube.com/watch?v=AS_5Cm695jU; TheACTUALWORLDNEWS, 2013) and discuss students' personal experiences with earthquakes. During this discussion, seek to make explicit clarifications to students' prior knowledge.

Guided practice

Show the YouTube video on how to use the P and S wave time travel graph and examples of how to use the graph ("Earth Science Reference Table Pg 11—P and S Wave Chart-Hommocks Earth Science Department"; metfan869, 2009). Show how P and S waves look/compare by using a "scientific slinky." Use the graph to connect to past learning in earth science and algebra.

Collaborative practice

Orchestrate a pair-and-share activity in which students work in pairs on a worksheet of problems. One student reads the problem while the other solves it, alternating roles between even and odd problems.

Closing

Prompt P and S wave comparisons from different pairs of students. Ask each student to summarize velocity and distance covered for either the P or S wave and then compare them verbally.

Extensions

In addition to making your specific objectives (content and language) visible to students by displaying them on the classroom's "Daily Agenda," you can also post the lesson online for students' perusal and reference. To do so, consider using the free school-to-home communications website, SchoolNotes (new.schoolnotes.com). As such, ELs will have the option to review key vocabulary and prepare for the lesson in advance.

Caveats

Though the potential for using visuals in language-content instruction is clearly demonstrated in the teachers' lesson on earthquake waves, several caveats are worth considering. First and foremost, teachers need to keep in mind that mere proximity

Name: _____

Using the Earthquake P-wave and S-wave Travel Time, please answer the following questions:

1. How long will it take for a P wave to travel 4,000 km? _____

2. How long will it take for an S wave to travel 6,000 km? _____

3. How far will a P wave travel in 4 minutes? _____

4. How far will an S wave travel in 19 minutes? _____

5. How far can an S wave travel in 4 minutes? _____

6. How far can a P wave travel in 8 minutes? _____

7. How far can an S wave travel in 7 minutes? _____

8. How long does it take for an S wave to travel 7,000 km? _____

9. How long does it take for a P wave to travel 6,000 km? _____

10. How long does it take for an S wave to travel 5,000 km? _____

11. How far can an S wave travel in 10 mins? _____

12. How far will a P wave travel in 10 mins? _____

13 How long does it take for a P wave to travel 8,000 km? _____

14. How long does it take for an S wave to travel 8,000 km? _____

15. How far can an S wave travel in 6 minutes? _____

16. How far can a P wave travel in 6 minutes? _____

17. How long does it take for a P wave to travel 3,000 km? _____

18. How long does it take for an S wave to travel 3,000 km? _____

19. How long does it take for an S wave to travel 9,000 km? _____

20. How long does it take for a P wave to travel 9,000 km? _____

Bonus: What seismic wave travels at a faster rate (P or S wave)? _____

Figure 2. Worksheet of problems used for pair-and-share activity.

to visuals does not necessarily support EL learning; teaching content with visuals requires, among other things, (1) strong organizational skills to preselect appropriate and sufficient images to complement instruction; (2) a solid understanding of images' roles in language/content instruction; (3) a solid understanding of appropriate mediational strategies to optimize the use of images; (4) skill in instructional pacing so that visual integration is seamless yet salient; (5) cross-cultural visual literacy to understand representations in the cultures of students, and students' representations of the host culture; (6) metalinguistic awareness to avoid potentially confounding colloquial language regarding visuals; and (7) skill to determine the most salient aspects of a visual, especially as it pertains to the topic at hand. Second, integration of language and content teaching at the secondary level is in its relative infancy. Much additional research that examines the interplay of images and effective teacher mediational strategies is needed.

Assessment and Evaluation

Give students an exit ticket—a quiz upon the bell to leave the classroom (Figure 3).

Name: _____

Earthquake Quiz:

Please answer the following questions using page 11 in ESRT.

1. How far can a P-wave travel in 4 minutes? _____
2. How far can an S-wave travel in 4 minutes? _____
3. How long does it take for a P-wave to travel 4,000 km? _____
4. How long does it take for an S-wave to travel 6,000 km? _____
5. What seismic wave travels faster (P-wave or S-wave)? _____

Figure 3. Exit ticket.

Reflection on and Analysis of the Lesson

The timing of the lesson worked well. Students remained consistently focused and on task. All but one student achieved a perfect score on the exit quiz. The teaching team noted the value of their collaborations and how they appreciated one another's support and assistance throughout, especially for Kate, who was able to focus on content knowing her peers were supporting the ELs' learning of the material. Dorothy (the ESL teacher) praised Kate for making salient connections for the learners on which she could build. For example, Kate showed why one wave is always below the other while comparing it to a road race between her and her students. She also asked students to imagine the effects of an earthquake in the classroom, which helped students relate the lesson to their own lives. There were moments, however, when Kate used idiomatic expressions which may have been problematic. For instance, while discussing the graph in Figure 1, Kate said something was "right on the money," though she immediately provided her meaning and said "right on the line." ("How long does it take a P wave to travel 2,000 kilometers? Well, we go into the graph with what you know. So 2,000 kilometers you go up to P, it crosses right on the money, I would say right on the line, right? So four minutes?"). She also asked about a "fault" line, and because there was not a visual to accompany this, the meaning was unclear. The video used challenging vocabulary, like *vertical* and *horizontal axis*, *independent* and *dependent variable*. It was unclear whether the ELs understood these terms. This underscores the challenges of having appropriate visuals at hand so as to maintain the instructional rhythm. Advancing teacher visual literacy in conjunction with their learning about the ELs in their classrooms is a must and virtuoso use of the interactive whiteboard is a promising direction in this regard (Meskill & Oliver, 2018).

During planning, the team focused a great deal on incorporating visual activities into each lesson. Kate reported having grown professionally from the experience and by having new understandings about language and the use of visuals. Nora, the preservice teacher, reported learning firsthand the challenges content vocabulary and concepts hold for ELs and praised her mentors for addressing these effectively with visual strategies.

This chapter extends the original case study in the anchor chapter (Oliveira & Weinburgh, 2016) in several respects. First, it strengthens our evidential basis for the importance of visual aspects of content-language integration in the specific context of multimodal science classrooms. The preceding testimonials and descriptions provide clear evidence that, when thoughtfully and systematically used, pictorial supports constitute important mediators of EL learning outcomes in integrated science-language instruction. Second, this chapter supports the contention that teacher engagement with research can indeed transform classroom practice in significant ways. As previously described, exposure to the anchor chapter on guided visualization (Oliveira & Weinburgh, 2016) enabled our teachers to purposefully improve the visual design of a science lesson, making it more conducive to EL mastery of scientific content and academic language. As such, this chapter takes an initial step toward answering the larger question of how to best visually support ELs in content-language integrated science classrooms. Our best answer at this time is careful visual scaffolding wherein instructional focus oscillates between abstract and concrete levels at critical moments of a lesson.

In addition to showing that there may be ways for high school teachers to make more systematic use of visuals in support of ELs, this chapter also points to potentially fruitful directions for future research. How such multimodal practices might be thoughtfully integrated through different programs of professional development constitutes one direction. Additionally, to more clearly and systematically characterize teachers' pedagogical deployment of pictorial supports in science as well as the associated impact that their practices produce on ELs, future studies can make use of eye-tracking devices. Preliminary studies reveal that visuals that include text in a foreign or second language give rise to unique patterns of eye movement (Plass, Chun, Mayer, & Leutner, 2003). Further, eye-movement data can provide highly accurate measurements of cognitive load (Rayner, 1998; Van Gerven, Paas, Van Mërrienboer, & Schmidt, 2004). Such a methodological approach would allow educators to quantitatively track ELs' cognitive load levels throughout content-language integrated lessons as they engaged with particular sequences of visuals. In short, our hope is that both researchers and practitioners will consider the role of multimodal enhancement in light of the rich instantiation we present.

Alandeom W. Oliveira is associate professor of science education in the Department of Educational Theory and Practice, State University of New York, Albany, USA.

Luciana C. de Oliveira is professor and Chair of the Department of Teaching and Learning at the University of Miami, Florida, USA.

Carla Meskill is professor of language and technology in the Department of Educational Theory and Practice, State University of New York, Albany, USA.

References

Chua, H. F., Boland, J. E., & Nisbett, R. E. (2005). Cultural variation in eye movements during scene perception. *Proceedings of the National Academy of Sciences of the United States of America, 102*(35), 12629–12633.

Fisher, D., & Frey, N. (2008). *Word wise and content rich: Five essential steps to teaching academic vocabulary*. Portsmouth, NH: Heinemann.

Garrison, L., & Mora, J. K. (1999) Adapting mathematics instruction for English language learners: The language-concept connections. In L. Ortiz-Franco, N. G. Hernandez, & Y. De La Cruz (Eds.), *Changing the faces of mathematics: Perspectives on Latinos* (pp. 35–48). Reston, VA: National Council of Teachers of Mathematics.

Gerena, L., & Keiler, L. (2012): Effective intervention with urban secondary English language learners: How peer instructors support learning. *Bilingual Research Journal, 35*, 76–97.

Goodwin, C. (1997). The blackness of black: Color categories as situated practice. In L. B. Resnick, R. Säljö, C. Pontecorvo, & B. Burge (Eds.), *Discourse, tools and reasoning: Essays on situated cognition* (pp. 111–140). Berlin, Germany: Springer.

Graves, M. F., August, D., & Mancilla-Martinez, J. (2013). *Teaching vocabulary to English language learners*. New York, NY: Teachers College Press.

Hansen, L. (2006). Strategies for ELL success. *Science and Children, 43*(4), 22–25.

Hite, C. E., & Evans, L. S. (2006). Mainstream first-grade teachers' understanding of strategies for accommodating the needs of English language learners. *Teacher Education Quarterly, 33*, 89–110.

Honigsfeld, A., & Dove, M. G. (2010). *Collaboration and co-teaching: Strategies for English learners*. Thousand Oaks, CA: Corwin.

Kress, G., & van Leeuwen, T. (2006). *Reading images: The grammar of visual design* (2nd ed.). New York, NY: Routledge.

Meskill, C., Mossop, J., & Bates, R. (1999). *Electronic text and English as a second language environments* (Vol. 12012). National Research Center on English Learning & Achievement, University at Albany, State University of New York. Retrieved from http://www.albany.edu/cela/reports/meskill/meskillelectronic12012.pdf

Meskill, C., & Oliver, G. (2018). English learners, academic content and classroom technologies: Multimodal amplifications at the intersection. Manuscript in preparation.

metfan869. (2009, December 14). *Earth science reference table pg 11—P and S wave chart— Hommocks earth science department* [video file]. Retrieved from https://www.youtube.com/watch?v=GcqSj43evE0

Nisbett, R. E., & Masuda, T. (2003). Culture and point of view. *Proceedings of the National Academy of Sciences of the United States of America, 100*(19), 11163–11170. doi:10.1073/pnas.1934527100

Nisbett, R. E., Peng, Choi, I., & Norenzayan, A. (2001). Culture and systems of thought: Holistic versus analytic cognition. *Psychological Review, 108*(2), 291–310.

New York State Education Department. (2012a). *NYS bilingual common core initiative: Theoretical foundations*. Albany NY: EngageNY. Retrieved from https://www.engageny.org/file/135506/download/nysbcci-theoretical-foundations.pdf

New York State Education Department. (2012b). *NYS bilingual common core Initiative: Teacher's guide to implement the bilingual common core progressions*. Albany NY: EngageNY. Retrieved from https://www.engageny.org/file/135511/download/teachers-guide-to -implement-the-bilingual-cc-progressions.pdf

New York State Education Department. (2013). *Physical setting/earth science: Core curriculum*. Retrieved from http://www.p12.nysed.gov/ciai/mst/pub/earthsci.pdf.

Oliveira, A. W., & Weinburgh, M. H. (2016). Guided visualization: Promoting ELL science literacies through images. In L. C. de Oliveira (Ed.), *The Common Core State Standards for literacy in history/social studies, science, and technical subjects for English language learners: Grades 6–12* (pp. 91–106). Alexandria, VA: TESOL Press.

Paivio, A. (1971). *Imagery and verbal processes*. New York, NY: Holt, Rinehart, & Winston.

Plass, J. L., Chun, D. M., Mayer, R. E., & Leutner, D. (2003). Cognitive load in reading a foreign language text with multimedia aids and the influence of verbal and spatial abilities. *Computers in Human Behavior, 19*(2), 221–243.

Quigley, C. F., Oliveira, A. W., Curry, A., & Buck, G. (2011). Issues and techniques in translating scientific terms from English to Khmer for a university level text in Cambodia. *Language, Culture and Curriculum, 24*(2), 159–177.

Rayner, K. (1998). Eye movements in reading and information processing: 20 years of research. *Psychological Bulletin, 124*, 372–422.

Reed, S. K. (2010). *Cognition: Theories and application* (8th ed.). Belmont, CA: Wadsworth Cengage Learning.

Sternberg, R. J. (2003). *Cognitive theory* (3rd ed.). Belmont, CA: Thomson Wadsworth.

Sturken, M., & Cartwright, L. (2009). *Practices of looking: An introduction to visual culture*. New York, NY: Oxford University Press.

Swanson, P. E. (2010). The intersection of language and mathematics. *Mathematics Teaching in the Middle School, 15*, 516–523.

Sweller, J. (2010). Element interactivity and intrinsic, extraneous, and germane cognitive load. *Educational Psychology Review, 22*(2), 123–138.

TheACTUALWORLDNEWS. (2013, July 22). *Earthquake rescue continues in China's Gansu province* [video file]. Retrieved from https://www.youtube.com/watch?v=AS _5Cm695jU

Van Gerven, P. W. M., Paas, F., Van Merriënboer, J. J. G., & Schmidt, H. (2004). Memory load and the cognitive pupillary response in aging. *Psychophysiology, 41*, 167–174.

Young, E., & Marroquin, C. (2008). Mathematics on the playground. *School Science and Mathematics, 108*, 279–283.

Section 4

Language Arts

Scaffolding the Language of Mathematics: Multiple Representations of Functions in Algebra

Geraldine Devine, Suzanne Toohey

Introduction

Since 2010, approximately 40 U.S. states have adopted the Common Core State Standards for Mathematics (CCSSM; NGA & CCSSO, 2010). With the adoption of the CCSSM, school districts are implementing instructional materials that focus on students' active participation in processing and producing the language of mathematics as they develop conceptual and procedural content knowledge. The CCSSM "demand that mathematics teaching and learning move from procedural and symbol manipulation exercises to concept-rich tasks deeply embedded in context that focus on students' sense making and understanding" (Kinch & Winicki-Landman, 2015, p. 71). As a result of the language required to build and communicate the deep mathematical understanding required by the CCSSM, English learners (ELs) need scaffolded linguistic supports to process and produce the language of mathematics.

To access and process the linguistically complex discourse in the secondary mathematics classroom, ELs need multiple, regular, and repeated opportunities to read, write, listen, and speak throughout the instructional cycle. Historically, mathematics instruction in the United States has been focused on skills and procedures taught through lecture and rote memorization (Stigler, Gonzales, Kawanka, Knoll, & Serrano, 1999). On the other hand, the National Research Council (2001) defines mathematical proficiency beyond merely procedural fluency, to include four additional strands: conceptual understanding, strategic competence, adaptive reasoning, and productive disposition.

The lesson described in this chapter is designed for the beginning of a ninth-grade Algebra course to introduce functional relationships and ways in which functions can be represented. The discrete steps of representing a geometric pattern numerically, and eventually algebraically, provide a foundation from which students create meaning about functional relationships. Students will apply the general ideas of functional relationships from this first unit, as they develop deeper understanding of specific function families (e.g., linear, exponential, quadratic), throughout the rest of the course.

The linguistic scaffolds developed for this lesson focus on creating meaning about functional relationships rather than the discrete steps involved in creating algebraic rules. First, students note the changing numerical expressions in a growing pattern. Then, the connections between representations empower students to make meaning. A deep understanding of the academic vocabulary associated with the representations is necessary for all students to communicate their understanding and make connections among multiple representations.

The context for this chapter is a suburban high school with approximately 850 students, Grades 9–12. Seventy-three percent of the students are economically disadvantaged. Approximately 30% of the students in the school are classified as ELs. Spanish, Arabic, and Hmong are the top three languages spoken by the school's ELs, respectively. Twenty percent of non-ELs and 14% of ELs have identified disabilities and receive special education services. The rich diversity of the student population in this classroom provided a vibrant context for our model lesson.

Synopsis of Original Research

Kinch, D., & Winicki-Landman, G. (2015). Creating waves in high school mathematics. In A. Bright, H. Hansen-Thomas, & L. de Oliveira (Eds.), *The Common Core State Standards in mathematics for English language learners: High school* (pp. 71–90). Alexandria, VA: TESOL Press.

The CCSSM requires students to employ deep mathematical understanding and sense making through linguistically complex tasks. The standards state, "one hallmark of mathematical understanding is the ability to justify, in a way appropriate to the student's mathematical maturity, why a particular mathematical statement is true or where a mathematical rule comes from" (NGA & CCSSO, 2010, p. 4). This represents a shift to explaining mathematical reasoning, which requires students to have command over not only mathematical skills, but also the ability to process and produce English at high levels of sophistication.

The CCSSM provide guidelines for what every student should know and be able to do in mathematics and English language arts from kindergarten through 12th grade. However, only a short supplemental guide directs teachers with rudimentary information about meeting the needs of ELs. It gives a rationale; it explains *why* it is important to maintain rigorous content expectations for ELs. In contrast, *The Common Core State Standards in Mathematics for English Language Learners: High School* (Bright, Hansen-Thomas, & de Oliveira, 2015) is a robust resource, providing practical guidance and detailed examples to assist teachers when implementing the CCSSM in classrooms with ELs. Several exemplar lessons are included, which demonstrate how to plan and facilitate deep, rigorous content learning with ELs. The chapter "Creating Waves in High School Mathematics" (Kinch & Winicki-Landman, 2015) was used as a model for the lesson described in this chapter; it illustrates how to implement rigorous mathematics learning while providing appropriate language scaffolds for ELs.

All teachers of ELs are responsible for teaching both language and core content (Office of English Language Acquisition, n.d.). For ELs to find success in the secondary mathematics classroom, teachers must attend to the unique language learning needs of their ELs by planning responsive and explicit language instruction. Responsive instruction purposefully plans for opportunities that engage ELs in reading, writing, listening, and speaking about mathematics. These opportunities encourage "growth beyond literacy and mathematics" and help "students to learn to communicate and collaborate as 21st-century citizens" (Kinch & Winicki-Landman, 2015, p. 72).

Additionally, responsive instruction for ELs requires teachers to consider how to reduce the linguistic complexity of a task without reducing the cognitive demand of the task. There is a relationship between the cognitive and linguistic demands embedded within a mathematical task. Often, as the cognitive demand of the mathematics task increases, so does the linguistic demand. ELs attempt to negotiate these demands in two or more languages. Secondary mathematics teachers should consider, and intentionally account for, the linguistic demand of mathematical tasks for both ELs and non-ELs. To do this, the authors of the anchor chapter encourage teachers to use "language as a tool for teaching and learning" (Kinch & Winicki-Landman, 2015, p. 74). Incorporating a variety of tools, such as instructional strategies, scaffolds, and supports, to make the language of mathematics more linguistically accessible, is one way teachers can compensate for linguistic complexity in a particular mathematics task.

For example, reducing the linguistic complexity of a reading task can unlock the meaning of the task for ELs and provide them an opportunity to develop and demonstrate conceptual understanding. Students need conceptual understanding of a word problem to use strategic solving approaches. A proper conceptual understanding of the problem requires students to make meaning from both mathematical and contextual words to interpret what problem solving approach is necessary and efficient. Strategies to assist ELs in processing language to develop this conceptual understanding and problem solve include attending to keywords, modifying language complexity, and using manipulatives.

ELs also need tools and high-leverage strategies to scaffold and support their production of mathematical language in order to participate in mathematical discourse. Tools such as sentence frames, sentence stems, and sentence models aid in production of mathematically precise, authentic English language production in writing or when speaking. When students work together and engage during the inquiry part of the lesson, the teacher may provide sentence frames and sentence stems to facilitate ease of oral communication between students. As students collaborate and develop claims, the role of the teacher is to "facilitate and encourage as peers probe and prod to elicit from the student or group of students what their evidence is for each claim" (Kinch & Winicki-Landman, 2015, p. 78). Providing students with tools to support their language production facilitates both productive and receptive language growth. As their "receptive language grows" so "does their ability to produce oral and written explanations" (p. 81). Without explicit instruction and significant language scaffolding, linguistic complexity presents a nearly impossible barrier to the overall comprehension of unit content.

ELs can find great success in the secondary mathematics classroom when they are provided with necessary scaffolds and supports for both processing and producing the English language. This success can translate into positive educational dispositions throughout the school experience. "With the appropriate teacher support together with peer and teacher interactions, all high school students, in particular ELLs, have the opportunity to process their understanding in more meaningful ways and have access to more cognitively demanding tasks" (Kinch & Winicki-Landman, 2015, p. 81). High-leverage strategies, language scaffolds, and opportunities to collaborate with peers provide different pathways to success for ELs in the secondary mathematics classroom.

Rationale

The following quote was the impetus for collaborating to create a well-scaffolded, appropriately accommodated algebra lesson about functional relationships:

> To move from a mindset of bubbling in the right answer to one guided by the standards for mathematical practice (MPs), more open-ended thinking from *all* the members of the classroom should be encouraged. For this to occur, mathematical discussions need to be a classroom staple. For classrooms including ELLs, this becomes even more important. ELLs have a dual learning goal; they must gain proficiency in the complexities of English as well as learn grade-level mathematics content. (Kinch & Winicki-Landman, 2015, p. 71)

Although the lesson described in this chapter does not present an idea wave, it relies on the philosophical underpinnings of the idea wave introduced in the anchor chapter. In this lesson, students will see a growing geometric pattern composed of squares and connect the pattern to numerical, and then abstract representations. It is through this inquiry that students begin to develop an understanding that as one variable changes, another variable changes because of it (i.e., a functional relationship). This lesson uses a purely mathematical context and does not situate itself in a real-life application. Subsequent lessons in this unit continue to utilize multiple representations, including real-world contexts. Real-world contexts provide a scaffold for the learning of new and complex mathematical concepts.

Traditionally, teachers often front load and define mathematical terms and concepts (e.g., *function, domain, range*) that students will encounter in an upcoming lesson without providing students with the chance to explore or inquire first. This approach does not give ELs a context in which to frame the learning of new terms. An inquiry-based alternative is to provide students with opportunities to develop a connected understanding to these ideas and encounter new concepts in rich tasks that incorporate multiple representations. These representations not only build conceptual understanding but also provide access to sense making and language production. Research and mathematical standards strongly support the use of multiple representations to develop conceptual understanding (e.g., National Council of Teachers of Mathematics, 1989; National Research Council, 2001). Like the Idea Waves lesson described in detail in "Creating Waves in High School Mathematics" (Kinch & Winicki-Landman, 2015), our lesson builds "on the idea there are multiple ways to represent mathematical ideas, with the intent that students switch between the representations flexibly" (Kinch & Winicki-Landman, 2015, p. 74). Students' ability to switch between representations flexibly is dependent upon their ability to process and produce the linguistically complex language associated with the topic of the lesson, Functional Relationships in Growing Geometric Patterns.

Lesson Plan

Lesson Plan Title	Functional Relationships in Growing Geometric Patterns
Grade/Subject Area	Grade 9; Algebra 1
Duration	1 hour
Proficiency Levels	WIDA (2012): All levels (Entering to Reaching)
Content and Language Objectives	Students will be able to • identify and describe, using words and algebraic expressions, the relationship between the independent and dependent values of a function in a growing geometric pattern. (Content) • write, or speak, in complete sentences in order to describe the relationship between values of a function. (Language)
Alignment to Standards	**Common Core State Standards for Mathematical Practice** (NGA & CCSSO, 2010) • *F-IF.4*: (Interpreting Functions) For a function that models a relationship between two quantities, interpret key features of graphs and tables in terms of the quantities, and sketch graphs showing key features given a verbal description of the relationship. • *F-BF.1.a*: (Building Functions) Determine an explicit expression, a recursive process, or steps for calculation from a context. • *CCSS MATHEMATICAL PRACTICE 6*: Attend to precision. • *CCSS MATHEMATICAL PRACTICE 7*: Look for and make use of structure. • *CCSS MATHEMATICAL PRACTICE 8*: Look for and express regularity in repeated reasoning.
Outcomes	Students will use structure in geometric patterns to represent, algebraically and in words, a functional relationship.
Materials	• Chart paper and markers or document camera • Colored pencils • Growing Geometric Patterns handout (Appendix, available on the companion website for this book) • Dot Pattern

Highlighted Teaching Strategies

We have developed supports throughout the lesson to scaffold language processing and production for learners across the levels of English language proficiency. When developing the supports and scaffolds, we made every effort to maintain the cognitive demand of the mathematics.

Suggested and required word lists

Both suggested and required word lists are recommended supports used to scaffold language production in the speaking and writing parts of this lesson. These particular supports should be utilized after the inquiry phase of the lesson, in which students authentically encounter the words and after you explicitly facilitate defining and repeatedly clarify the use of each mathematical and contextual word included in the word list(s).

Suggested and required word lists are low-prep strategies designed to promote productive language development. The required word list is an excellent tool for ELs at higher proficiency levels, cueing them to use the expected language for the task. It also aids both ELs and non-ELs to use precise mathematical language when speaking and writing for mathematical purposes. We gave ELs at WIDA (2007) Levels 5 and 6, as well as non-ELs, a required word list, and ELs at WIDA Levels 1–4 a suggested word list during the lesson exploration.

Sentence frames/stems/models/language prompts

In this lesson, sentence stems and language prompts for speaking and writing are provided to all students during the number talk routine and to WIDA (2007) Levels 1 and 2 ELs on the exit ticket. During the lesson launch, the sentence frames and language prompts alert all students to the language expected to meaningfully participate in the whole-group discussion. Sentence frames and models provide the scaffolding necessary to help ELs move from dependent to independent writers and speakers, over time.

Partner or small-group work

Within this diverse, language-rich mathematics classroom, students are continually engaged in partner and small-group work. This lesson affords students the opportunity to interact orally with others during each step of the instructional cycle. In this instance, you have purposefully paired ELs at WIDA (2007) Levels 1 and 2 with ELs at higher levels of English language proficiency as they are exploring patterns on the Growing Geometric Patterns sheet.

Pointing and gesturing

During the lesson launch, you and your students point and gesture to communicate. Students gesture to explain the structure that they notice in a particular pattern. Likewise, students point to "top" or "bottom" and/or point to a geometric shape as they move from recognizing structure in one figure to generalizing those features in any figure. This activity gives students the opportunity to develop Standards of Mathematical Practice 7 and 8 (NGA & CCSSO, 2010).

Concrete representations

The concrete representations in both the dot pattern warm-up and the Growing Geometric Patterns handout equip students with a visual representation from which numerical representations can be developed. As the figures in the pattern grow, students use regularity and repeated reasoning to identify what stays the same and what changes. Students use this information to write an abstract equation, which could be used to find the number of squares for any figure number, or independent variable.

Differentiated product

Carefully consider scaffolding language production to differentiate the expected product, so that all learners are engaging in rigorous and appropriate mathematical reasoning. For example, on the Growing Geometric Patterns handout, Question 3 asks students to "explain how to draw any figure in the pattern." WIDA (2007) Level 1 ELs might explain through drawing, labeling, and using single words. ELs at WIDA Levels 2 and 3 might use simple sentence frames, such as "First, draw _____" and/or "For figure ____ I would draw a _____ with _____." We caution you, however, when constructing similar sentence frames not to give away strategies and thus prescribe a particular solution. ELs at WIDA Levels 4+ could be required to use transition words and/or prepositions of location (e.g., *at the top, to the right, adjacent to*) when answering this question.

Think-pair-share

The common think-pair-share routine (Lyman, 1981) gives students the opportunity to use and refine language with a partner before participating in the whole-group discussion.

Procedures

There are two primary connected components in this lesson: an opening number talk (Humphreys & Parker, 2015) and an inquiry activity, Functional Relationships in Growing Geometric Patterns. For this lesson, the number talk revolves around a dot pattern (see Figure 1 for examples). Show a pattern made of dots for a few seconds, so that students attend to the structure of the image to reason about the total number of dots rather than counting individual dots. Wait for students to signal that they have ideas they are ready to share.

After significant wait time, students call out the total number of dots as you document their numerical responses on the board. (It is important to note that all answers are accepted, so that students can use the subsequent conversation about how they arrived at the totals to critique their own reasoning and the reasoning of others.)

Next, facilitate a conversation about the strategies students used to find the total. To scaffold the language demand and support concept development, create a table on a large poster. The first column should have the sentence stem "I saw . . . ," and the language prompt "_____ groups of _____" in the header row and several copies of the dot pattern in the rows below the header. Subsequent columns are labeled "expanded form," "simplified expanded form," and "total."

To begin the conversation, utilize the think-pair-share strategy and invite several students to share their thinking. Subsequently record students' strategies on the poster (see Figure 1 for a completed poster). To wrap up the number talk, ask additional questions to highlight the usefulness of different forms of the equations (i.e., expanded form, simplified form) and problem-solving strategies (e.g., attending to structure) that students could utilize in the Functional Relationships in Growing Geometric Patterns activity.

I saw... ____groups of ____	Expanded Form	Simplified Expanded Form	Total
"I saw 4 hockey sticks" "4 groups of 4"	4 + 4 + 4 + 4	4(4)	16
"I saw 3 diagonals and 4 dots" "4 groups of 3 and 4"	3 + 3 + 3 + 3 + 4	4(3)+ 4	16
"I saw 4 on top, 4 on the bottom, twos in the middle" "2 groups of 4 and 4 groups of 2"	4 + 4 + 2 + 2 + 2 + 2	2(4) + 4(2)	16
"I saw [gesture inverted v with hands]" "2 groups of 5 and 2 groups of 3"	5 + 5 + 3 + 3	2(5) + 2(3)	16

Figure 1. Dot pattern warm-up completed example.

The second part of the lesson, taking up the majority of the class time, engages students in collaborative problem solving as they explore the Functional Relationships in Growing Geometric Patterns handout (see Figure 2). In the launch, note that the column headers on the new sheet are the same as those on the poster students co-constructed in the dot pattern. Using the dot pattern as an example, also clarify the meaning of newly encountered vocabulary (i.e., *same/constant, changing/varying*) that students will use during the task.

In the inquiry phase of the task, students work in small groups as you listen to their conversations, ask clarifying and probing questions to assess and deepen student thinking, and collect student thinking anecdotally for the whole-group debrief. (See Figure 3 for an example of student work.)

Closing

To close the lesson, facilitate a whole-class conversation that highlights concepts, strategies, and academic vocabulary. To draw attention to main ideas and related vocabulary being discussed, write the suggested and required words *vary/constant, independent/dependent,* and *expression* on the board. As student teams present each

Engaging Research: Transforming Practices for the High School Classroom

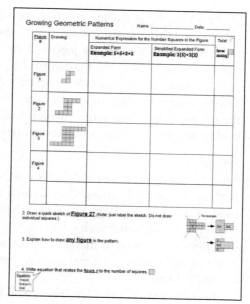

Figure 2. (a) Growing geometric patterns handout (b) Growing geometric patterns handout with supports to scaffold the language demand.

Figure 3. Examples of student work from the lesson summary.

of the strategically chosen solution strategies, ask students to identify parts in the expressions that remain constant and others that vary. Give students opportunities to identify how the *varying* pieces of the expressions, eventually represented by a *vari*able, are related to the figure number.

With just a few minutes left in class, ask students to work in their small groups to complete an exit ticket in which they identify and describe, in complete sentences, the relationship between the independent and dependent values of the function they explored in the growing geometric pattern.

Extensions

An interesting extension for this lesson would be to create an idea wave in which students are actively engaged in writing about mathematics. "An idea wave can be used to develop crucial mathematical habits of mind" (Kinch & Winicki-Landman, 2015, p. 73). Students seeing themselves as mathematicians and developing a positive disposition toward mathematics is an example of a crucial mathematical habit of mind and a theme throughout the standards for mathematical practice (NGA & CCSSO, 2010).

An Idea Wave activity has three main parts:

> In the first part, the students are asked to consider what the teacher
> has written about a particular idea, graph or picture, and then to write
> two or more statements of their own about the idea. The second
> part . . . asks students to work individually to complete the given
> sentence starters around the mathematical ideas being discussed. The
> final step . . . is to have the student pairs share their ideas with others.
> (Kinch & Winicki-Landman, 2015, p. 75)

The idea wave incorporates similar language scaffolding and supports as the lesson outlined here. However, the focus is on writing, using the language of mathematics. The idea wave is an excellent extension to the Functional Relationships in Growing Geometric Patterns lesson.

This lesson could also be extended to introduce specific families of functions (e.g., linear, quadratic, exponential; see Figure 4).

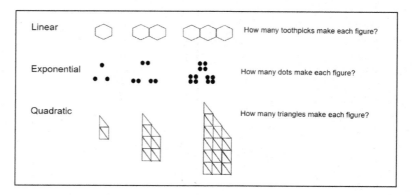

Figure 4. Patterns to introduce function families.

Students investigate patterns that illustrate distinguishing characteristics of that family. New terminology (e.g., *common ratio*, *exponential*, *second difference*) could be introduced from the concrete investigation that would be used more abstractly in following lessons.

Caveats

Secondary mathematics teachers typically have highly specialized training in advanced mathematics but may lack training in literacy and second language acquisition. When designing accommodations for ELs, the secondary mathematics teacher faces many challenges. One challenge that presented an issue when developing this lesson was avoiding overscaffolding, and intentionally leaving out scaffolds and supports that reduced the demand of the mathematics or changed the rigor of the mathematics for ELs at WIDA (2007) Levels 1 and 2, primarily. In providing linguistic simplification, teachers can inadvertently change the mathematical nature of a problem from utilizing multiple representations for sense-making and problem-solving to focusing on discrete steps. Furthermore, teachers can overscaffold mathematics tasks, thus reducing the cognitive demand of the tasks and eliminating students' opportunities to reason and problem solve.

There are many resources available to assist the secondary mathematics teacher in designing appropriate language scaffolds and supports without undermining the rigor of the mathematics task. First, the WIDA Instructional Framework (WIDA, 2012) is an important resource for all teachers of ELs; specifically, the Performance Definitions and Model Performance Indicators help teachers develop background knowledge about English language proficiency. The Performance Definitions help the secondary mathematics teacher better understand expectations of language development and skills based on students' levels of language proficiency. Likewise, the Model Performance Indicators provide examples of differentiation, by content area, across the levels of language proficiency. To view additional high-quality strands of differentiation with corresponding supports, mathematics teachers should explore the "DRAFT Language Supports" documents embedded within the Michigan Association of Intermediate School Administrators mathematics units, Grades 3 through Geometry (Michigan Association of Intermediate School Administrators and Oakland Schools, n.d.).

Pacing of a lesson is another challenge in the diverse mathematics classroom. A teacher needs to attend closely to pacing and make related instructional decisions based on both the goals of the lesson and students' understanding of those goals. An important aspect of pacing inquiry lessons (Michigan State University, n.d.) is allocating time for three phases of a lesson. In the first 5–10 minutes, the teacher activates students' prior knowledge, introduces mathematical and real-life contexts, and generates engagement. In the second phase of the lesson, students collaboratively grapple with rich mathematical ideas and build meaning through problem-solving. The teacher closely monitors student thinking and collaboration to highlight in the summary. The final summary stage is imperative. In this whole-class conversation, the teacher focuses student thinking on the important ideas of the lesson and reiterates students' progress toward the goal. The class also analyzes the efficiency of individual strategies and makes generalizations.

In the Functional Relationships in Growing Geometric Patterns lesson, it is possible that not all students will have completed the entire set of problems by the end of the class period. However, you can move to the whole-class summary if students have done enough of the inquiry to engage in the discussion. Additionally, you might choose to partition the summary into parts, where some of the discussion is continued the following day. The summary of this lesson should facilitate students beginning to recognize how using regularity and repeated reasoning can help move from representing individual figures in a pattern to using an algebraic expression to represent any figure. Providing students discussion time, as a whole class, to compare different strategies and related equations helps nurture that skill development.

At the same time, there are valuable functional ideas that this activity addresses. Ideas such as independent variables, dependent variables, and functions need to be highlighted. There may not be sufficient time in small groups and whole-class discourse for students to make sense of and answer this prompt:

> *Identify and describe, in complete sentences, the relationship between the independent and dependent values of a function in a growing geometric pattern.*

If there is insufficient time, you can move this prompt and related conversations to a subsequent day.

Assessment and Evaluation

Assessment is formative and ongoing throughout the lesson. Student learning is measured as you listen to rich conversation as it is happening in pairs, small groups, and the whole group. Evaluating mathematical sense-making requires you to both watch and listen. Newcomer ELs may point and gesture to ask questions and communicate their understanding. It is important that you closely watch and document, formally or informally, evidence of student understanding throughout the lesson. Allowing students to use multiple modes of communication when reasoning about representations ensures that students have many different methods of demonstrating what they know and can do. In sum, Kinch and Winicki-Landman (2015) emphasize "the need to listen to what the students are saying. If you ask a question and the answer is not what you are looking for, look again. Listen to the mathematics in what the student is saying. It may not be precise, but the thinking you are hoping for may be there—hidden, but there" (p. 72). Evaluate the intent of an EL's answer rather than the precision.

At the conclusion of this lesson, revisit the original objectives and conduct a whole-group reflection of the language objective, "describe the relationship between values of a function by writing or speaking in complete sentences." Next, ask students to individually reflect on whether or not they accomplished the intentions of the content objective by completing an accommodated exit ticket prompt:

- ELs at WIDA (2012) Levels 1 and 2 are orally asked, "What is the independent variable? What is the dependent variable?"; and are given an exit ticket with the following sentence frames:

— The independent variable is _____.

— The dependent variable is _____.

- Non-ELs and ELs at WIDA (2012) Levels 3+ are given the following exit ticket:

  — What is the independent variable? What is the dependent variable?

  — _____ is a function of _____.

Reflection on and Analysis of the Lesson

Throughout the lesson, the students engaged in multiple opportunities to develop deep understanding of the mathematical concepts related to functional relationships through exploration of multiple representations. Throughout the instructional cycle of this lesson, students constructed, coordinated, and made sense of representations collaboratively. For example, in the lesson, the teacher noted a couple of places on the Functional Relationships in Growing Geometric Patterns handout where a group of students at Table A exhibited incomplete mathematical understanding.

Figure #	Drawing	Expanded Form	Simplified Expanded Form	total
1		2 + 2 + **1**	2 (2) + **1**	5
2		4 + 4 + **4**	3(4)	12
3		6 + 6 + **9**	2 (6) + **9**	21
4		8 + 8 + **16**	2 (8) + **16**	25
n				

Figure 5. Student thinking from Table A.

First, the expression 3(4) for Figure #2 in the simplified expanded form did not follow the pattern of reasoning documented for their other figures (i.e., $2(2) + 1$, $3(4), 2(6) + 9, 2(8) + 16$). As a result, the teacher facilitated a conversation at the table that both scaffolded revision and also named the standard for mathematical practice that would assist this revision.

Teacher: What do you think we mean by "regularity in repeated reasoning"? [placing a notecard with this standard on their table. Long pause.] How about the word *repeat*?

Student 1: To do something more than once.

Student 2: Over and over again.

Teacher: Okay, let's look at the expressions you have in this column. Does your reasoning, your thinking, repeat?

Student 2: Not really.

Student 3:   Maybe without this one [pointing at 3(4)].

Teacher: [modeling the use of precise mathematical language] So, you are saying the *expression* 3(4) doesn't follow the pattern of the other *expressions*, like 2(6) + 9? What do others think about that?

Each member of the table group contributed to a revision that more concretely showed a pattern. The teacher then began to address the second issue she noticed. Namely, the numerical expressions did not clearly relate to the figure number. To generate a need to rewrite the expressions again, the teacher asked the students to use the patterns in their expressions to find the total number of squares for the fifth figure.

Student 3:   It would have two groups of 10, but then what?

Student 2:   Wait, how do you know two groups of 10?

Student 3:   Look. Two times two, two times four, two times six, two times eight. What comes next?

Student 2:   Oh. Two times 10.

Student 1:   Okay, but what do we do with these 1, 4, 9, 16?

[Pause]

Teacher: What hints can you get from that part of the figure?

Student 2:   That part of the figure is a square.

Student 1:   Yea! So, we can do two squared, three squared, and five squared.

Teacher: Will you write the symbols you just described on the recording sheet for your partners to see what you said?

Watching her teammate write the expressions, Student 3 noted, "Figure one has one squared. Figure two has two squared. Figure five has five squared. Figure eighteen would have eighteen squared."

Teacher: What you just did was to determine the square term from the independent variable, the figure number. You are beginning to use the relationship between the figure number [gesturing to the first column] and the number of squares [gesturing to the simplified expanded form column]. See if you can do that for the first part of the expressions, too. As you work together, see if you can use words from our word bank.

Throughout the lesson, all students had the opportunity to engage in deep and rigorous learning.

The strategies and examples of deep and rigorous learning illustrated in the exemplar lessons within *The Common Core State Standards in Mathematics for English Language Learners: High School* (Bright et al., 2015), had great influence on our practice. From the onset of our collaborative efforts, we strongly connected with the following statement:

Because so much of mathematics content can be made visible and concrete, mathematics experiences in school have the potential to serve as a kind of "on-ramp" for engagement with the school experience, providing a ready sense of success. . . . Mathematics is a ready and capable mode through which English itself may be taught and learned. (2015, p. 2)

This lesson illuminated the high level of engagement in mathematics learning that occurs for students across all levels of English language proficiency when they are able to access the content through appropriate scaffolds and supports. This engagement provides a ready sense of success with the potential to spread across the school experience.

Adding an explicit language objective at the start of the lesson and an unplanned language objective within the lesson provided an authentic way to teach and learn English. Through a well-timed mini-lesson on prepositions of location, the teacher provided deliberate, authentic, and task-based instruction on a language-dependent skill, which helped students persevere through challenging mathematical processes. What follows is a description of what happened during the mini-lesson:

> At Table B, the teacher noticed that students had not used prepositions of location (e.g., *adjacent to*, *on top*) in their written directions. Although the directions the students generated were not mathematically incorrect, the teacher used this opportunity to engage students in a mini-lesson to increase mathematical precision. Using prepositions of location to describe the figure could be a secondary language objective for some students.

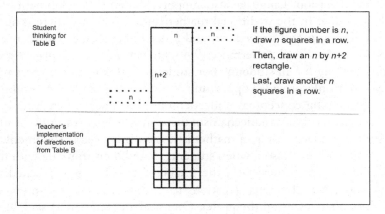

Figure 6. Student thinking from Table B.

The teacher asked students at Table B to take turns reading directions to draw the squares for Figure #6 on the Growing Geometric Patterns handout and said:

Teacher: I'll draw what I hear you describing on my grid dry erase board. The rest of the group, quietly pay attention to what you are hearing and assess two things. One, how well am I following directions? And two, what changes will make your directions clearer?"

The exchange started smoothly.

Student 1: Draw six squares in a row [with a horizontal gesture].

[The teacher produced the correct visual.]

Student 2: Draw a 6 by 8 rectangle.

S2 did not clarify where to draw the rectangle. So, the teacher intentionally drew the rectangle in the wrong position to illustrate what happens when prepositions of location are omitted.

Student 3: Draw six squares *on the top right*.

The teacher then produced the visual which corresponded with mathematically precise student directions.

Finally, the teacher posed the following questions for students at Table B to contemplate on their own and discuss with one another as students continued to revise their written directions. "Why did including this preposition of location feel important? Are there other places in your directions where prepositions of location might be helpful?" Watching several heads nod, the teacher asked the group to make revisions and left to interact with other groups.

As a result of the successful use of this mini-lesson on prepositions of location, we intend to be more purposeful in developing mini-lessons on targeted explicit language skills in our unit design process and guidance for teachers.

In this conversation, the teacher identified ways in which language could increase mathematical precision. Language also supports students' development of conceptual understanding. In the traditional mathematics classroom, there is an overemphasis on calculation and procedures and a deemphasis on language use (Stigler, Gonzales, Kawanka, Knoll, & Serrano, 1999). However, language plays a pivotal role in meaning making for all students. For students in this lesson, discussing the dot pattern task not only provides opportunities to develop academic vocabulary, it is a tool for developing conceptual understanding. For the teacher, listening to and engaging in conversations is a mechanism through which she carefully scaffolds and assesses student understanding of mathematics and language development.

For example, in this lesson, when students shared their thinking with the whole group during the dot pattern task, the teacher listened closely, restated students' responses, and asked clarifying questions to understand and document students' unique solution strategies on the poster. One student (Student 1) said, "I saw four hockey sticks." The teacher asked for clarification, to which the student gestured and articulated, "There are three dots that make the stick, and one for the blade."

Teacher: So each hockey stick is a group of four?

Student 1: Yes.

Teacher: Would someone be willing to use this frame [pointing to the language prompt "____groups of____"]?

Student 2: Yea. Four groups of four.

This particular conversation illustrates how students use informal language and sense making from familiar contexts, like hockey sticks, to communicate within mathematical contexts. Intentional questions and established routines in the classroom help bridge students from this more common language to language that is mathematically precise.

Similarly, during the lesson, the teacher recognized that WIDA (2012) Level 1 ELs needed additional direction to complete Problem 3, so she provided accommodated directions during her walk around and asked a non-EL speaker of the same first language to provide directions in that language. Furthermore, during this investigation, a WIDA Level 1 student was able to draw and gesture to a rectangle on the Growing Geometric Patterns handout but was unable to name the shape. A WIDA Level 3 student, working with the WIDA Level 1 student, was able to name the shape for the Level 1 student.

Three areas of further research came to the forefront as we planned and executed this lesson:

1. What possible impacts might color coding have on EL comprehensibility of mathematical discourse? This question arose for us when creating the dot pattern warm-up and the summary of Functional Relationships in Growing Geometric Patterns activity. In both cases, the teacher color coded the dot groups and geometric patterns to correspond to the expressions in the Expanded Form and Simplified Form columns. This helped students point, talk, and gesture to and about the groups; the color coding scaffolded students' language production and connection among representations.

2. What are effective methods for training secondary mathematics teachers on English language proficiency and differentiating mathematics content for ELs? We continue to struggle with how to involve secondary mathematics teachers in ongoing, job-embedded professional learning targeting better practices for engaging ELs in secondary mathematics. This is especially challenging in districts with low-incidence populations of ELs. Where the compelling need exists, all teachers are motivated to learn how to differentiate for ELs.

3. How might the cooperative group routines developed in research about complex instruction (Stanford University, n.d.) prevent ELs from "hiding" in the mathematics classroom? In our lesson, ELs are continuously engaged in conversation about the mathematical content. However, when ELs are not required to speak in the mathematics classroom, the teacher may not be able to determine students' true abilities. During complex instructional routines, the teacher "trains the students to use cooperative norms and specific roles to manage their own groups" (Stanford University, n.d.). Complex instruction requires all students to work interdependently to solve problems (Stanford University, n.d.).

The appendix for this chapter is available at www.tesol.org/practices-highschool.

Geraldine Devine is a mathematics education consultant at Oakland Schools, Waterford, Michigan, USA, a regional service agency.

Suzanne Toohey is an ESL/Title III consultant at Oakland Schools, Waterford, Michigan, USA, a regional educational service agency.

References

Bright, A., Hansen-Thomas, H., & de Oliveira, L. (Eds.). (2015). *The Common Core State Standards in mathematics for English language learners: High school*. Alexandria, VA: TESOL Press.

Humphreys, C., & Parker, R. (2015). *Making number talks matter developing mathematical practices and deepening understanding, grades 4–10*. Portland, ME: Stenhouse.

Kinch, D., & Winicki-Landman, G. (2015). Creating waves in high school mathematics. In A. Bright, H. Hansen-Thomas, & L. de Oliveira (Eds.), *The Common Core State Standards in mathematics for English language learners: High school* (pp. 71–90). Alexandria, VA: TESOL Press.

Lyman, F. (1981). *The responsive classroom discussion: The inclusion of all students*. In A. S. Anderson (Ed.), *Mainstreaming digest* (pp. 109–113). College Park, MD: University of Maryland College of Education.

Michigan Association of Intermediate School Administrators and Oakland Schools. (n.d.). *Oakland schools atlas rubicon curriculum management system*. Retrieved from https://oaklandk12-public.rubiconatlas.org/Atlas/Public/View/Default

Michigan State University. (n.d.). *Connected mathematics project*. Retrieved from https://connectedmath.msu.edu/classroom/getting-organized/pacing/

National Council of Teachers of Mathematics. (1989). *Curriculum and evaluation standards for school mathematics*. Reston, VA: Author.

National Governors Association Center for Best Practices (NGA),& Council of Chief State School Officers (CCSSO). (2010). *Common Core State Standards for mathematical practice*. Washington, DC: Authors.

National Research Council. (2001). Adding it up: Helping children learn mathematics. Washington, DC: National Academies Press. doi:10.17226/9822

Office of English Language Acquisition. (n.d.). *English learner toolkit*. Retrieved from https://www2.ed.gov/about/offices/list/oela/english-learner-toolkit/index.html

Stanford University. (n.d.). *Program for complex instruction*. Retrieved from http://cgi.stanford.edu/group/pci/cgi-bin/site.cgi

Stigler, J. W., Gonzalez, P. A., Kawanka, T., Knoll, S., & Serrano, A. (1999). *The TIMSS videotape classroom study: Methods and findings from an exploratory research project on eighth-grade mathematics instruction in Germany, Japan, and the United States*. Washington, DC: NCES.

World Class Instructional and Design and Assessment. (2007). WIDA's 2007 English Language Proficiency Standards, grades 6–12. Retrieved from https://www.wida.us/standards/eld.aspx

World Class Instructional and Design and Assessment. (2012). WIDA 2012 Amplification of The English Language Development Standards. Retrieved from https://www.wida.us/standards/eld.aspx

Conclusion

Holly Hansen-Thomas, Mary Amanda Stewart

In the final chapter of her collaborative work with García, *Translanguaging With Multilingual Students*, Kleyn (2016) outlines important implications for high school and other level teachers and teacher educators in "setting the path" to work with emergent bilinguals. Some of the key lessons Kleyn presents are building a classroom community inclusive of all students' languages and cultures; lesson planning that includes more than just content knowledge, but that also encompasses students' linguistic strengths and challenges; and ensuring that the linguistic landscape of the classroom and the school is reflective of students' home languages and cultures, as well as the content they need to know (pp. 203–204). Though these are just a few suggestions from a long list, they are reflective of current research and practice and are crucial to inclusive and meaningful education in the high school classroom. Many of these key lessons have been manifested in various ways in high school classrooms in the current volume.

Engaging Research: Transforming Practices for the High School Classroom has addressed a variety of innovative pedagogical concepts, such as guided visualization, argumentation, genre pedagogy, translanguaging, accountable talk, and use of graphic organizers and picture books. In clear, insightful, and very practical ways, the contributing authors have shown how high school teachers can use previously published TESOL research to enhance and enrich their practice with their multilingual learners.

We see this volume as a practical, hands-on guide that specifically English language arts, social studies, science, and mathematics—and even other content areas outside of the core—high school teachers can use to stay current about second language teaching research, and to adapt those key concepts into practice in their own classroom. We hope, and indeed expect, that it will be a transformative guide to the professional development of high school teachers of ELs, and that their students will benefit in multiple ways from these lessons and activities designed especially for them.

Reference

Kleyn, T. (2016). Setting the path: Implications for teachers and teacher educators. In O. García & T. Kleyn (Eds.), *Translanguaging with multilingual students: Learning from classroom moments* (pp. 202–220). New York, NY: Routledge.

Appendix: Anchor Texts

Section 1: Language Arts

Chapter 1. Approaching Argumentation Playfully in the English Language Arts Classroom

> Giouroukakis, V., & Honigsfeld, A. (2010). High-stakes testing and English language learners: Using culturally and linguistically responsive literacy practices in the high school English classroom. *TESOL Journal, 1,* 470–499. doi:10.5054/tj.2010.240193

Chapter 2. El Cucuy and the Boogeyman: A Multicultural Arts-Based Approach to Poetry

> Cahnmann-Taylor, M., Bleyle, S., Hwang, Y., & Zhang, K. (2017). Teaching poetry in TESOL teacher education: Heightened attention to language as well as to cultural and political critique through poetry writing. *TESOL Journal, 8,* 70–101. doi:10.1002/tesj.263

Chapter 3. Translanguaging to Support Reading and Writing Engagement in the English Language Arts Classroom

> Daniel, S. M., Jiménez, R. T., Pray, L., & Pacheco, M. B. (2017). Scaffolding to make translanguaging a classroom norm. *TESOL Journal.* Advance online publication. doi:10.1002/tesj.361

Section 2: Social Studies

Chapter 4. Breaking Through: Using Authentic Literature to Teach Social Studies

> Short, D. J., Fidelman, C. G., & Louguit, M. (2012). Developing academic language in English language learners through sheltered instruction. *TESOL Quarterly, 46,* 334–361. doi:10.1002/tesq.20

Chapter 5. Picture This! Using Illustrated Books to Support Comprehension of Social Studies Complex Texts

> Palincsar, A. S., & Schleppegrell, M. J. (2014). Focusing on language and meaning while learning with text. *TESOL Quarterly, 48,* 616–623. doi:10.1002/tesq.178

Chapter 6. From Research to Practice: Equipping English Learners With History Literacy Skills

> Schall-Leckrone, L. (2017). Genre pedagogy: A framework to prepare history teachers to teach language. *TESOL Quarterly, 51*, 358–382. doi:10.1002/tesq.322

Section 3: Science

Chapter 7. Bilingual Biomes: Revising and Redoing Monolingual Instructional Practices for Multilingual Students

> Cummins, J. (2009). Multilingualism in the English-language classroom: Pedagogical considerations. *TESOL Quarterly, 43*, 317–321. doi:10.1002/j.1545-7249.2009.tb00171.x

Chapter 8. Transforming Language and Content in Science Learning for Secondary English Learners

> Ardasheva, Y., Howell, P. B., & Vidrio Magaña, M. (2016). Accessing the classroom discourse community through accountable talk: English learners' voices. *TESOL Journal, 7*, 667–699. doi:10.1002/tesj.237

Chapter 9. On Shaky Grounds: Teaching Earthquake Science to English Learners Through Guided Visualization

> Oliveira, A. W., & Weinburgh, M. H. (2016). Guided visualization: Promoting ELL science literacies through images. In L. C. de Oliveira (Ed.), *The Common Core State Standards for literacy in history/social studies, science, and technical subjects for English language learners: Grades 6–12* (pp. 91–106). Alexandria, VA: TESOL Press.

Section 4: Mathematics

Chapter 10. Scaffolding the Language of Mathematics: Multiple Representations of Functions in Algebra

> Kinch, D., & Winicki-Landman, G. (2015). Creating waves in high school mathematics. In A. Bright, H. Hansen-Thomas, & L. de Oliveira (Eds.), *The Common Core State Standards in mathematics for English language learners: High school* (pp. 71–90). Alexandria, VA: TESOL Press.